HERE TO HELP:

UFOs AND THE
SPACE BROTHERS

HERE TO HELP:

UFOs AND THE
SPACE BROTHERS

GERARD AARTSEN

Here to Help: UFOs and the Space Brothers
First published December 2011
2nd edition, December 2012

Photo credits:
Page vi: Photographer or copyright-holder unknown. Pages 54, 57 and 100-103: Photographer(s) or copyright-holder(s) unknown. Reproduced from books published by Alberto Perego in 1958 and 1963, in the interest of UFO research. Page 72: Still photograph by Pablo Dessy from video footage by Mónica Coll, © analuisacid.com. Pages 94-95 and 107: Photographers unknown. Reproduced with permission from *Share International* magazine. Pages 58 and 120: Photographer(s) or copyright-holder(s) unknown.

ISBN-13/EAN-13: 978-90-815495-3-0

Published by BGA Publications, Amsterdam, the Netherlands.
www.bgapublications.nl

Typeset in Calisto MT.

Cover design: Jan Henkes.

Cover photograph:
Space craft near the city of Malargüe, Mendoza, Argentina, in one of seven photographs taken by Félix Fernández, early April 2008.

This book is written
in service to Brothers and Sisters,
everywhere.

On 17 February 2010 the *Rajasthan Times* reported that intricate prehistoric cave paintings depicting extraterrestrials and UFOs were found in caves hidden deep within dense jungle in the Hoshangabad district of Madhya Pradesh, India, near the local administrative centre of Raisen. According to information coming from Benjamin Creme (*Share International* magazine, June 2010) the cave art, which depicts a man from Mars, a saucer-type craft, and a force field or trail, was painted 40,000 years ago.

Contents

List of illustrations

Preface

Taking its cue from the Ageless Wisdom teaching, which posits the evolution of consciousness as the purpose of life, on Earth or anywhere else, this book brings together ample evidence of the attempts of the space visitors to show humanity an alternative to the age-old ways of competition and greed that have brought our world to the brink of annihilation.

Since no number of sightings seems sufficient to counter the general disbelief in the reality of the space people generated by the disinformation campaign that governments initiated in the 1950s, I will attempt to present the evidence in such a way that it helps the reader to connect dots that he was possibly not aware of before, even if that challenges the beliefs he has held thus far.

After having established that the extraterrestrial presence is a fact, we will first look at the destructive effects which the early cover-up has had on the general perception of the UFO phenomenon and on subsequent attempts to uncover the truth. For a clear understanding of the purpose of the extraterrestrial presence on Earth we will also look at the conspiracy theories which have resulted from these cover-ups and provide evidence to unravel them once and for all.

We will then take a closer look at the state of the world and the systems and institutions that are crumbling as we write, continuing to present a broader reality through testimonies of contactees past and present, substantiated by the work of ground-breaking thinkers.

We will learn of several consistent and related attempts by the space people in different parts of the world to help us gain a broader, more spiritual understanding of life, including practical ways in which they have been supporting humanity, mostly unbeknown to the world, by sharing their technology.

Finally, we will see that the coming of the UFOs is not an event in itself, but occurs in support of that major transition which humanity is currently undergoing. While there is no lack of popular thought-forms about the form this transition will take, including "ascension", "the opening of interdimensional portals", "the arrival of extradimensional beings" et cetera, its true nature will be shown to be at once less fanciful and more profound.

Our governments possess large amounts of information and evidence which activists are pressuring them to disclose, but confirmation of the reality of the UFOs and the space people may take a wholly different form of 'disclosure' than currently advocated or expected by most UFO enthusiasts.

In all likelihood, an announcement from our governments that they know about the visitors from space, and have known about them since the 1940s, will not happen before mankind begins to give expression to the essential human values that we are now beginning to reconnect with on a global scale, in response to the crescendo of greed that has seized the world in a deadly grip. As we will see, the UFOs are here to help, as humanity comes into its own and decides on the future of our planet and our lives.

Amsterdam,
November 2011

Acknowledgements

The author wishes to express his gratitude to Anna Spiga in Scotland and Horacio Londner in Spain for their help with Italian and Spanish sources respectively, and to Adrie van Dijk in Holland for his help with the photographs. The author is also greatly indebted to Benjamin Creme in England, for his untiring elaboration of the Ageless Wisdom teachings.

1. The extraterrestrial presence

As the number of increasingly spectacular UFO sightings around the world continues to grow, so too does the number of retired or active government officials and other dignitaries who go on the record with their experiences of other-worldly craft or beings, as well as the number of relatively high-profile happenings that indicate the world's readiness to hear the truth about the presence of UFOs on our planet.

After years of struggling to be given access to government files and have witnesses' statements recognized or validated, a global 'exopolitics' movement is now a fact. The efforts of many individuals, groups and organizations seem to be bearing fruit in a convergence of events that indicate the cover is no longer big enough to cover up the truth.

As a result, even mainstream science has started publicly, albeit tentatively, to investigate again the prospect of human interaction with extraterrestrial life. In 2010 the Royal Society of London on two separate occasions organized debates concerning contact with life from elsewhere in the universe. In January 2010 the Society held discussions about the consequences for science and society of the detection of extraterrestrial life, followed in October by four panel debates that tackled the same question from different angles.[1] The debate titled 'Extraterrestrial life and arising political issues for the UN agenda' was attended by the head of the United Nations

Office for Outer Space Affairs (UNOOSA), Mrs Mazlan Othman. A Malaysian astrophysicist, Professor Othman was heralded in some media as the UN appointed ambassador for "extraterrestrial affairs", to which she responded: "I am not about to be appointed the ambassador to aliens [but] it would make sense for the United Nations and its member states to study the important question of who should represent humanity if aliens do come to this planet."[2]

The global business community, too, is joining the fray. In January 2011 the Saudi-sponsored Global Competitiveness Initiative in Riyadh featured a panel discussion titled "Contact: Learning from Outer Space" at which UFO researchers Stanton Friedman, Nick Pope and Jacques Vallée helped an audience of world business leaders obtain a sense of the possibilities that would open up if contact with extraterrestrials were established[3], although it remains to be seen if the motives of the space people coincide with their own, as we will discuss in later chapters.

More importantly, though, an increasing number of government officials and military experts whose credibility and integrity cannot be denied are going on the record to inform the world of their first-hand observations. The year 2010 saw two major events in this respect.

One was the publication of Leslie Kean's book *UFOs: Generals, Pilots and Government Officials go on the record*, which is based on official documents that the author gained access to under the Freedom of Information Act through an initiative which she launched in 2001 with the help of John Podesta, the fourth White House Chief of Staff under President Bill Clinton. She shows how the US government has created public distrust by neglecting – some would argue, actively debunking – this crucial topic.

The other one happened on 27 September 2010, when an

unprecedented press conference took place at the National Press Club in Washington DC, which was reported by mainstream media around the world. In this press conference seven former United States Air Force personnel testified to the existence of UFOs and their ability to neutralize or disengage nuclear missiles. UFO researcher Robert Hastings, who organized the conference, said: "I believe (...) this planet is being visited by beings from another world, who, for whatever reason, have taken an interest in the nuclear arms race which began at the end of World War II."[4] He stated that the seven officers at the conference were among a group of around 120 former military officials who all had similar experiences.

Former USAF nuclear missile launch officer Robert Salas in particular did not mince his words when he spoke about the role of the US military in the cover-up: "The US Air Force is lying about the national security implications of unidentified aerial objects at nuclear bases and we can prove it." He feels the extraterrestrials were sending a message, literally shining a light on nuclear weapons: "They could have done a lot more damage, permanent damage, to our weapons systems, and they didn't. If they wanted to destroy them, with all the powers they seem to have, I think they could have done that job, so I personally don't think this was a hostile intent."

Hastings believes that the US government is withholding information about UFOs for fear of mass panic, but, he argues, the people should be allowed to decide for themselves what to believe. "The (...) people have a right to know the facts. This is a national security issue but it is [also] a need-to-know issue, a right-to-know issue. Citizens in every country on Earth should be let in on this secret."[5] While discussing the events during the live CNN coverage, eyewitnesses seemed still as impressed or moved as they were when they first witnessed them.

While highly significant in that so many former government and military eyewitnesses who cannot and are not generally dismissed as tinfoil hat fruitcakes finally speak out about their own experiences, the focus here is still on proving the reality of the UFOs.

And in the face of so much indisputable evidence and so many undeniable testimonies I do not think there is much to add in this respect – anyone who insists on denying the fact of these extraordinary craft that continue to be recorded almost daily in ever greater numbers and detail, is clearly a victim of the criminal cover-up that governments and the military have perpetrated on behalf of major political and economic interests since the subject first gained worldwide attention in the 1940s and 1950s. Alternatively, they suffer from the blinkered prejudice of mainstream science which, aided by the corporate-beholden media, prefers to ignore any facts which do not fit its particular template of reality, rather than broaden its scope through unbiased, proper research of the unknown.

The approach taken in this book, therefore, differs from other books in that it is written from the understanding that UFOs are real and testify to the fact of the universality of life as the Cause, rather than the haphazard result of a chemical accident in the backwaters of cosmos; and that our planet has always been visited by these interplanetary craft and their crew, increasingly so since the discovery of nuclear fission technology during the Second World War of the previous century and its application in nuclear weapons and power stations.

Instead, when so many witnesses with backgrounds in government, the military, aviation and astronautics come forward to state, based on their own experience, that the extraterrestrial presence on Earth is real, the next logical question concerns the purpose of their presence and their intentions and that is what this book will address.

The consensus among exopolitics experts and disclosure advocates seems to be that we are being visited by a variety of extraterrestrial races with different agendas and, as usual in today's world, the more disturbing reports seem to draw the most attention and, often, credulity.

In contrast, however, the early contactees brought an unequivocal message of hope. Orfeo (Orville) Angelucci, for instance, was told by his space contacts in 1952: "We feel a deep sense of brotherhood toward Earth's inhabitants because of an ancient kinship of our planet with Earth. In you we can look far back in time and recreate certain aspects of our former world. With deep compassion and understanding we have watched your world going through its 'growing pains'. We ask that you look upon us simply as older brothers."[6]

Wilbert B. Smith, who from 1950-1954 was the director of Project Magnet, a UFO study programme that was authorized by the Canadian Department of Transportation, and himself a contactee, said in 1958: "The [space] people tell us of a magnificent Cosmic Plan, of which we are part, which transcends the lifetime of a single person or a nation, or a civilization, or even a planet or a solar system. (…) We are told of the inadequacies of our science and we have been given the basic grounding for a new science, which is at once simpler and yet more embracing than the mathematical monstrosity, which we have conjured up."[7]

Likewise, George Adamski, who wrote about his contacts in *Flying Saucers Have Landed* (1953) and *Inside the Space Ships* (1955), said in 1958: "Their appearance is in accordance with the Universal Plan of brotherhood, wherein they offer a helping hand and words of counsel in time of need; a situation Earth finds itself in today."[8]

Many people, including UFO researchers, have always

understood that the coming of the UFOs would have profound effects on the way we run our world, especially as a result of the new technologies which have or will become available through the study of crashed craft and interaction with the occupants. What many do not seem to realize, however, is that these changes will not be limited to the outward structures of our lives.

In June 1947, in an assessment of the possible implications of an extraterrestrial visitation of Earth titled 'Relationship with Inhabitants of Celestial Bodies', Robert Oppenheimer and Albert Einstein wrote: "It is difficult to predict what the attitude of international law will be with regard to the occupation by celestial peoples of certain locations on our planet, but the only thing that can be foreseen is that there will be a profound change in traditional concepts."[9]

Astronomer and cosmologist Dr Carl Sagan has been quoted as saying: "On the day that we do discover that we are not alone, our society may begin to evolve and transform in some incredible and wondrous new ways." But while his famed TV-series *Cosmos* espoused the empiricists' doctrine of life as the most "precious form of matter"[10], the 'incredible and wondrous' changes which Sagan foresaw for society are in essence to do with a realignment of humanity with the spiritual realities of life that we sacrificed in the attempts to find 'truth' in the material aspect of our existence.

Fritjof Capra, the physicist and author, has been speaking out against that limited view of science, saying that "...all scientists have been tremendously influenced by the mechanistic and reductionist view that underlies classical physics and the general Western way of thinking. The method of reducing complex phenomena to basic building blocks and of looking for the mechanism through which these interact has become so deeply ingrained in our culture that it has often been identified with science itself and with the scientific method. Views, concepts, or ideas that did not fit into this framework were either not taken seriously, as in the case of mysticism or paranormal phenomena, or they were considered as psychotic, as in the case of spontaneous transpersonal experiences."[11]

Indeed, more than one contactee has intimated that the coming of the UFOs and the space people will mean the overhaul of our existing economic and social structures as a result of a profound change in our perception of life. For instance, George Adamski has said: "...our neighbors [in space] are willing to share their knowledge with us, if we are willing to do our part. They know that our viewpoint of life is based on false premises, and our present attitude and behavior will lead to self-annihilation."[12] Here he was obviously referring to mainstream science that has lent itself to debunk anything that does not fit the accepted notions of what is possible or real.

Likewise, the Italian contactee Giorgio Dibitonto was told: "...you have set matter and spirit against each other. (...) If you could free your mind from its presumptuous arrogance, and become meek and simple, pure and good (...) then you would solve the whole problem of evil and your unhappiness. The intellect becomes ensnared if it represses or subverts [the wisdom of the heart]. Then the heart and the mind become enemies of each other, and the result is all manner of misfortune and sickness..."[13] Even a quick look around the world confirms this assessment of the state of our planet and our lives.

Therefore, says George Adamski, "Their program is vast in scope, and the pattern well laid out. They do not judge us for our disbelief, for they know that in time all of this dilemma of fantasy will die of its own reality. And people of Earth will use their minds to think clearly and realistically, and mystery will be replaced by understanding of natural law."[14]

In order to reach a better understanding of what kind of changes to expect, in the next chapter we will first uncover the extent of the damage that the initial cover-ups have done, and recognize how that has led many people to accept a paradigm of fear as the backdrop for the UFO phenomenon. Rooted, as many of us are, in a strictly materialistic view of life we will need to become aware how an age-old sense of separation and division has allowed most people to act and respond from fear of 'the other' and the unknown, while the so-called 'learned' have nothing but disdain for anything that is not based on accepted reductionist practice.

This fear and disdain have grown to the point that, in the words of author Timothy Good, "It is now mandatory to scorn contactees, due in part to sometimes banal and evangelical messages imparted to them by the 'space brothers', and because the extraterrestrials they have encountered do not conform to preconceived notions of alien appearance, behaviour and origin."[15]

And while Mr Good made a case for the many accounts "from too wide a variety of sources and countries, all of which contain scientifically interesting data elements in common"[16], the current volume is rather meant to broaden the scope of the subject beyond the nuts-and-bolts by showing the many important connections and parallels that exist between the UFO phenomenon and the Ageless Wisdom teaching as handed down to humanity throughout the ages by the Men of Wisdom, both in terms of spiritual philosophy and its practical application in our daily lives.

Seen in this context, it will become clear that there is nothing 'banal' or 'evangelical' about the messages from space, advocating as they do socio-economic changes which would end the divisions that separate those who live well and those who starve unnecessarily, thereby giving expression, for the first time in human history, to the truth which everyone knows in his or her heart: that we are all intimately related to – and dependent on – the planet and each other.

Notes

1 See the Royal Society of London website: <royalsociety.org/Event.aspx?ID=1887> and <royalsociety.org/extra-terrestrial-life/> [Accessed 5 June 2011]

2 Gregory Katz (2010), 'UN Official denies she has a role representing Earth to extraterrestrials'. AP News, [online] 5 October. Available at <www.royalsociety.org.nz/2010/10/06/britain-alien/>. [Accessed 5 June 2011]

3 Global Competitiveness Forum website, <www.gcf.org.sa/en/>, [accessed 4 June 2011]; videos of the discussions can be watched here: <news.exopoliticsinstitute.org/index.php/videos-of-extraterrestrial-life-panel-for-business-leaders-released/1>.

4 Jason Hanna (2010), 'UFOs eyed nukes, ex-Air Force personnel say'. CNN newsblog *This Just In*, [online] 27 September. Available at <news.blogs.cnn.com/2010/09/27/ufos-showed-interest-in-nukes-ex-air-force-personnel-say/> [Accessed 5 June 2011]

5 Ledyard King-Gannett (2010), 'Former Air Force Officers Discuss Sightings'. *Air Force Times News*, [online] 27 September. Available at <www.airforcetimes.com/news/2010/09/ap-Former-Air-Force-officers-discuss-UFO-sightings-092710/>. [Accessed 5 June 2011]

6 Orfeo Angelucci (1955), *The Secret of the Saucers*, p.9

7 Wilbert B. Smith (1958), speech given 31 March in Ottowa, Canada. Transcript published in *Flying Saucer Review* Vol.9, No.5, September-October 1963, p.16

8 George Adamski (1957-58), *Cosmic Science for the promotion of Cosmic Principles and Truths*, Series 1, Part No.4, Question #64

9 Robert Oppenheimer and Albert Einstein (1947), 'Relationship with Inhabitants of Celestial Bodies'. Available at <www.majestic documents.com/pdf/oppenheimer_einstein.pdf> [Accessed 1 September 2011]

10 Carl Sagan (1980), *Cosmos: A Personal Voyage*, episode 1: 'The Shores of the Cosmic Ocean'

11 Fritjof Capra (1978), 'The New Physics and the Scientific Reality of our Time'. In David Lorimer (ed.; 1998), *The Spirit of Science – From Experiment to Experience*, pp.41-42

12 George Adamski (1964), 'The Space People'. In Gerard Aartsen (2010), *George Adamski – A Herald for the Space Brothers*, p.126

13 Giorgio Dibitonto (1990), *Angels in Starships*, pp.47-49

14 Adamski (1964), op cit.

15 Timothy Good (1998), *Alien Base – Earth's Encounters with Extraterrestrials*, p.2

16 Ibidem

2. From cover-up to conspiracy

The cover-up efforts that were first employed to the fullest following the initial publicity about the crash of a UFO near Roswell, New Mexico, USA in July 1947, and went into overdrive to contain and reduce the massive interest that was generated by the experiences and information coming from George Adamski and other early contactees, had much farther reaching insidious effects than merely setting back the awareness and acceptance among the general public of the extraterrestrial presence by several decades. Catering to the existing, at times perhaps healthy, distrust among the public of authorities, these cover-ups also spawned an infectious culture of suspicion as a result of which wild speculation now seems to be the standard method of 'research' and 'deduction' in the field of Ufology.

At the same time, those who assert to hold fast to scientific methods are not always helping much either. To some people, especially debunkers, skeptics and researchers who crave to be taken seriously, truth is only that which consists of facts that are based on empirical data.

Apart from the misleading notion that everything knowable can be measured, or that only the measurable is worth knowing, if everyone would follow this logic we might still be living in the dark ages of bloodletting as a cure-all. For how do you discover anything new if you are not willing to confront the unknown, which by its very nature is unmeasurable? Besides, in such a universe scientists would have no reason to spend millions of dollars on attempts to prove the existence of particles they 'know' must exist – because their calculations tell them that 96 per cent of the known universe is made up of it – except their instruments so far fail to register them. The conclusion must therefore be that – if we insist on a strictly materialistic world view – our ability to establish facts and, from these, truth depends largely on the sensitivity – or perhaps the suitability – of our instruments. But, of course, what our instruments fail to measure may still be real beyond the scope of the instruments.

Obviously, if we are to expand our understanding from what we know at any given point to include the first level above it, we need to work with hypotheses. And while it is important to think *outside* the proverbial box, especially given the prevalent arrogance of mainstream science, it is equally important not to stray too far from the box. This may be one of very few instances where I agree with zoologist and fundamentalist atheist Richard Dawkins, who says: "We should be open-minded, but not so open-minded that our brain falls out"[1] (although arguably some people's brain could do with some fresh air). In other words, any hypothesis needs to follow from – not remain within – what we know to be real or true, based on our existing knowledge and our own experience.

At the same time we should remember, as Carl Sagan admits in his 'baloney detection kit', that while, where possible, quantifying data makes it easier to discriminate between competing hypotheses for empirical purposes, "there are ... truths to be sought in the many qualitative issues we are obliged to confront, but finding them is more challenging"[2], especially if your instruments are not up to the task, we might add.

In order, then, to research anything that lies beyond what is already known, or what our 'instruments' are able to register or quantify, we cannot shy away from confronting such "qualitative issues", through verifying evidence from different independent sources where possible, and checking that any new information, teaching or hypothesis "follows sequentially upon that already offered"[3], as one teacher taught, "to enhance or corroborate an already known truth..." until it is either rejected or experienced in our own consciousness.[4]

Likewise, knowing that the more outrageous stories and claims usually generate the most interest, and that there are many people who have an overactive imagination or an insatiable need for attention in a world that celebrates celebrity for its own sake, it is all the more important to tread cautiously while discerning fact from fiction, with our shared traditions and our own experience as a starting point.

Life, a universal principle

As the source from which all the world's teachings have originated, the Ageless Wisdom tradition provides a solid and well-tested working hypothesis.

The notion that 'Life' is not the result of the evolution of form, such as documented by Darwin, but rather the Primal Cause of all there is, seeking ever more perfect expression of itself through the evolution of consciousness, was first introduced to a wider Western audience by Madame Helena P. Blavatsky (1831-1891). According to these hitherto esoteric Wisdom teachings man is not a biological being that has developed a spiritual aspect, but rather a spiritual being, an immortal Spark of the divine, that needs a vehicle (i.e. the personality) to experience the world and express itself. Life, therefore, is not limited to the solid physical plane of this planet on the fringe of our galaxy, but instead a universal *principle*, and the evolution of its expression does not stop with the human kingdom.

Various authors, including Mme Blavatsky, Baird T. Spalding, Alice A. Bailey, Rolf Alexander M.D., Murdo MacDonald-Bayne Ph.D., and George Adamski, have testified to the reality of the spiritual kingdom which has evolved out of the human kingdom and which is inhabited by the Masters and initiates of Wisdom of this planet, as the living proof of this ongoing evolution of consciousness, while reservations about the authenticity of their experiences are based on the fact that mainstream science is unfamiliar with – or unwilling to accept, even as a hypothesis – this notion of Life.

Allegorical and more literal evidence of the universality of this view of life, however, is found in the mythological and historical accounts, respectively, of the lives and precepts of the world's Teachers, such as Hercules and Hermes, Mithra, Vyasa, Krishna, the Buddha, the Christ, Shankara and Mohamed, to name some of the best known. Many of their teachings have subsequently become the basis for the world's major religions, while the long-standing connection between these religious traditions and extraterrestrial visitations was documented as early as 1953 by Desmond Leslie in his part of the book *Flying Saucers Have Landed*.

The same view finds further corroboration in the teachings of more contemporary Indian Avatars, such as Ramakrishna, Ramana Maharshi, Paramhansa Yogananda and Sathya Sai Baba, many of whom are considered divine incarnations of extraterrestrial origin, as well as in the teachings that have come from the space people through both early and later contactees, such as George Adamski, Wilbert Smith, Bruno Sammaciccia, Giorgio Dibitonto and Michael Wolf, among many others.

These Wisdom teachings, being the source of religious

traditions, and their more esoteric counterparts that were given through several disciples of the Masters of Wisdom, such as H.P. Blavatsky (HPB), Alice A. Bailey and more recently Benjamin Creme, throw a revealing light on the questions that have long perplexed many Western philosophers and scientists.

So, when researching claims of contactees or researchers, our first concern should be to see to what extent their experiences and any information that their space contacts convey coincide with the basic tenets of the teachings that have been set forth by the Guides and Teachers who have evolved out of Earth humanity and whose wisdom, even if distorted by intermediaries and the passing of centuries, has shaped civilizations and epochs.

While allowing for variations in details due to background, epoch and culture, together these teachings constitute an overwhelming body of evidence from a variety of sources in support of this hypothesis of Life, which renders it a solid and secure basis from which to move forward.

From the standpoint of the empirically-minded researcher, a lot of this will require acceptance as a working hypothesis first, before it is gradually experienced in one's own consciousness. And in his appeal to his audience or his readers it seems that esotericist Benjamin Creme really touches on the same qualitative challenge that Dr Sagan referred to (see p.12) when he says: "What I have to say is largely prophecy and cannot be proved. (...) All I ask is that you keep an open mind so that as the events take place, you will be less astonished, more in touch with the reality that is presenting itself to the world."[5]

As we allow this to happen, it explains ever more of the mysteries of the world – including near-death experiences, life after death, the nature of ghosts, ancient civilizations, or, indeed, the appearance of the UFOs in our skies that has been going on for centuries, if not millennia. At the same time, when authors or researchers make claims or provide explanations that ignore the tenets of this long-established tradition, for instance about the origin of man as outlined in the Wisdom teachings, and use speculations about extraterrestrial experiments or cross-breeding in, say, ancient Sumer as the basis for their research, we need not concern ourselves with questions about its validity. Such claims disregard humanity's most ancient records as documented in Blavatsky's magnum opus, *The Secret Doctrine,* which was written in close co-operation with the Masters of Wisdom, and a copy of which Albert Einstein kept on his desk for reference.[6]

And, should anyone still question the validity or relevance of HPB's work, given that she was 'revealed' as a fraud in a report by the Society for Psychical Research (SPR) in 1885, it actually turned out that the report was fraudulent and was therefore wholly and unequivocally retracted by the same SPR in 1986.[7] In fact, the more one reads HPB's own words, the more it becomes clear that she was indeed a seer, one of those people who can see somewhat further than the average man, as this riposte from 1890 to an adamant 19th century adherent of the 'Enlightenment' shows, which has not lost any of its currency in 2011:

"Our age, we say, is inferior in wisdom to any other, because it professes, more visibly every day, contempt for truth and justice, without which there can be no wisdom. (...) Because this century of culture and worship of matter, while offering prizes and premiums for every 'best thing' under the sun, from the biggest baby and the largest orchid down to the strongest pugilist and the fattest pig, has no encouragement to offer to morality, no prize to give for any moral virtue... Because, finally, this is the age which, although proclaimed as one of physical and moral freedom, is in truth the age of the most ferocious moral and mental slavery, the like of which was never known before. ... Rapid civilization, adapted to the needs of the higher and middle classes, has doomed by contrast to only greater wretchedness the starving masses."[8]

Similarly, it might be illuminating to know, in this respect, that throughout the years, through his contact and work with one of the Masters of Wisdom, Benjamin Creme has been predicting and advocating the very social changes that we are witnessing around us now, in preparation for the return to the everyday world of the Spiritual Hierarchy of Masters with the World Teacher for the new age at their head. In fact, in an article from July 1982 his Master wrote: "...over the last few years, great changes have been taking place in the world which herald a new dawn, a gradual transformation of society and its structures on a scale hitherto unknown. (...) The united voice of the people of all lands calling for justice and sharing will set up an invocation which nothing can resist. Thus will the world be transformed."[9]

Many other statements that Benjamin Creme has made over the years have proven correct. In May 2011, for instance, his announcement, made in 1979, that "below the area around the Great Pyramid and the Sphynx is a city, a colonial Atlantean city, which one day will be excavated and revealed"[10], received preliminary confirmation with the discovery, from satellite images, of an intricate ancient settlement, including 17 'lost' pyramids.[11]

Cover-ups, conspiracies and speculation
Seen from this wider perspective of Life and the evolution of consciousness, the coming of the UFOs could only be a hope-

inspiring event. How is it possible, then, one might ask, that so many people today see it as a threat?

As early as 1963 the Italian consul Alberto Perego had a good idea of what was going on. He wrote: "On 20 November 1952 (...) two [UFO] landings took place, one in North America, California and the other in South America, Brazil. On the same day, two men in the Americas were informed directly by extraterrestrial pilots, 'that other planets are inhabited; that a nuclear war on Earth would cause serious disruption in cosmos; and that the only purpose of the space ships was 'protective' and in the general interest'.

"This news was revealed simultaneously (and independently, as they did not know each other) by George Adamski in California, and Dino Kraspedon[12] in Brazil. The first was an amateur astronomer, the latter a physicist. These two men then became martyrs, being accused of forgery, vilified, discredited in every way, and derided by our 'scientists'! As a result, the world public opinion until today only vaguely knows what Adamski and Kraspedon have described in great detail.

"Before them, other 'civilians' had had contacts with disks and space pilots: Galbraith in Ontario (1948); Enrico Bossa in Argentina (1950); Daniel Fry in New Mexico (1950); Truman Bethurum in California (1952); Orfeo Angelucci in California (1952). But all were discredited and derided."[13]

As I have documented in my book *George Adamski – A Herald for the Space Brothers*, once Adamski had become world famous for the books in which he described his meetings and experiences with men and women from other planets in our solar system, the powers-that-be got seriously worried. Since he refused to be silenced or sidelined by offers of substantial sums of money or by intimidation, the mainstream media were enlisted to trivialize and ridicule Adamski and his experiences.[14]

As Adamski said during a press conference in September 1955 to promote his book *Inside the Space Ships*: "I was on Steve Allen's television show when I was in New York recently and I was told, 'Don't let anyone put words in your mouth. We've been told to play this whole thing down.' The man didn't say *who* told him."[15] These efforts were in fact so effective that he is still considered best to be ignored by many today.

Nonetheless, as Adamski's space contacts told him: "...your air forces and your governments *know* that our ships seen in your skies are from outer space, and that they can be made and piloted only by intelligent beings from other planets. Men high in the governments of your world have been contacted by us."[16] Canadian government researcher Wilbert Smith confirmed this, when he said: "...EVERY nation on this planet has been officially informed of the existence of the space craft and their occupants from elsewhere..."[17] This notion is further confirmed by many others, including Benjamin Creme, who says in his latest book: "The United States government, like all other governments, knows that the UFOs exist."[18]

These statements seem to be confirmed by the US government itself in the 1st Annual Report of the US President's Special Panel on UFO research (circa 1948), in a section called 'Government Policy of Control and Denial': "One of the most difficult aspects of controlling the perception in the public's mind of government attempts of denial and ignorance – is actual control of the press. Until a clear intent is established with diplomatic relations firmly at hand, it is the recommendation of the President's Special Panel with concurrence from MAJESTIC TWELVE, that a policy of strict denial of the events surfacing from Roswell, N.M., and any other incident of such caliber, be enforced. A inter-active program of controlled releases to the media, in such fashion to discredit any civilian investigation, be instituted in accordance with the provisions of the 1947 National Security Act."[19]

Majestic-12 was a group of 12 hand-picked individuals, 6 civilians and 6 military (2 from the army, the navy and air force each), who were assigned in the 1940s to gather as much information as they could about the extraterrestrial presence and intentions. While researching the authenticity of this group, UFO researcher Stanton T. Friedman discovered a government document in the US National Archives in College Park, Maryland, dated 14 July 1954, that has all the characteristics of an official government document, complete with watermarks and original declassification markings, which mentions "MJ-12" for the above-top-secret classification "Majestic-12" or "Majic-12", and which is important evidence to the reality of the Majestic-12 Special Studies Group.[20]

This government policy of concealment and derision was as much as admitted by the third director of the CIA, Vice Admiral Roscoe H. Hillenkoetter, when the *New York Times* of 28 February 1960 quoted him as saying: "It is time for the truth to be brought out in open Congressional hearings... [B]ehind the scenes, high-ranking Air Force officers are soberly concerned about the UFOs. But through official secrecy and ridicule, many citizens are led to believe the unknown flying objects are nonsense..."[21]

George Adamski, who was one of the first victims of the kind of large-scale debunking that resulted from these cover-up efforts, said: "I assure you the price for sharing this knowledge is indeed high. The skepticism and ridicule I have had to face makes it possible for me to sympathize with others who are reluctant to tell of their experiences with the visitors. It is ironical that this very disbelief has opened wide the doors for impersonations and falsifications, which only leads to more confusion. For these constant denials have kept the true facts from the public. So many, in their eager searching, have been misled regarding the normalcy of the space people. The same skepticism and ridicule has been instrumental in silencing our leaders concerning the facts they have been given by the interplanetarians."[22]

To be sure, Adamski was not alone in his experience. The Italian journalist Bruno Ghibaudi was working, in 1963, on a TV programme about people who claimed they had seen flying saucers or taken pictures. In an interview that year he said that this was no easy task "because so many people who had had these experiences or taken these pictures and had then spoken boldly about it, had either lost their jobs or been subjected to avalanches of ridicule and molestation, or hours of grilling by officialdom, and were now thoroughly sick of the whole thing and loath to open their mouths again."[23] In the event, the programme was cancelled, although Ghibaudi continued his investigation.

The decades-long cover-up and deliberate attempts on the part of governments to confuse and scare the public about the nature of UFOs and the space visitors, has infected even the community of people who have long struggled against the odds to wrest the truth from secretive government agencies and has led to ever wilder speculation. Since the character assassination on Adamski in the 1950s and 1960s, UFOs could no longer come from the other planets in our system, only from other galaxies. But of late that seems just one option and now even some of the more respected researchers in the field think it possible that UFOs originate from a secret society on Earth. One theory, if one can call it that, basically runs like this: "What if the Nazis or their successors succeeded in developing anti-gravitational technology to propel their secret spacecraft? Would it then not make sense that they used their technology to escape to some extraterrestrial location?" (Actually, no, it wouldn't.) Even the suggestion of a causal relationship then seems to suffice to carry the weight of the most outrageous speculations by researchers who should know that speculation does not equal research.

Given all the secret government and military operations to cover up the reality of the space visitors, this line of reasoning goes, there is every possibility that there is a 'breakaway civilization' who are keeping very advanced technology from the rest of us, and why would they not be planning to colonize the Earth for their own benefit?

A slight problem with this 'reasoning' is, of course, that the large majority of humanity and the largest part of the world's produce have *already* been 'colonized' by the very same economic interests that have done everything in their power to keep the public in the dark about the extraterrestrial visitors.

As early as the 1950s, Canadian researcher and contactee Wilbert Smith thought that politicians were reluctant to speak out about the true nature of the extraterrestrial visitors because they were afraid there was no public support for the subject of UFOs: "[B]ecause of the type of publicity from which the whole matter of flying saucers has suffered, politicians, who are naturally very sensitive to public reaction, are reluctant to stick their necks out."[24]

The reason for this negative publicity was clear to George Adamski, who told his Swiss contact Lou Zinsstag in 1955: "It is quite understandable, for the ones who control the press and all outlets of information fear the truth, so they keep it from the public the best they know how. They are the people that control the monetary system of the world."[25]

According to esotericist Benjamin Creme, who worked with the space visitors in the 1950s and has been in contact with one of the Masters of Wisdom since 1959: "There is an agency in the United States that has as its sole purpose the distortion of the reality of the UFOs,"[26] which has been active for over 60 years. "In this way, the people in control in, or even behind, the governments of the world retain their power,"[27] according to Creme. After all, he says, "It is ignorance and fear that drives the governments to act as they do. They understand that if humanity knew that the Space Brothers really existed, and these spacecraft with such a command of space and time really existed, we could ask them to help, because our governments obviously do not know what to do. They could advise and teach humanity. Who needs governments like we have today when we have these beneficent, harmless beings waiting to help us?"[28]

And so, in the 60 years since the truth about UFOs and the reality of the visitors from space began to be covered up and maligned, we have gradually gone from 'abductions' by malicious 'aliens' for the purposes of 'implanting' devices, 'experimenting' on humans, 'harvesting genes', 'breeding hybrids' as well as 'mutilating' cattle, to tracing the lineage of the houses of economic/financial power to a thousands of years old secret society of shape-shifting 'reptilians' of extraterrestrial or even indigenous origin, the so-called 'Illuminati' (or 'Nephilim', 'Anunnaki', depending on the conspiracy theory of your preference), who are working to subject humanity to their 'New World Order', while others are now seriously suggesting that there is reason to believe in a 'breakaway civilization' that is hiding somewhere in the solar system (on the moon?! Mars?), waiting for an opportunity to take over the Earth for their personal use – as if the economic and financial resources aren't already in the hands of the global elite.

The *new* world order?

Scary? That is exactly what cover-ups, secrecy and manipulation will do: engender suspicion leading to fear, which easily becomes irrational. And of the negative emotions, fear has proven to be the most infectious and self-strengthening. But none of the conspiracy theories that now abound among UFO enthusiasts and conspiracy theorists alike, which were spawned by corporations and the military conspiring to intimidate the early contactees into refraining from spreading their message of hope, would likely have reached this level of frenzy or fearfulness if they weren't based on some real-life facts – although mostly not of the kind that conspiracy theorists are looking for. Some of these facts, it would seem, have either been cleverly misrepresented or they were misunderstood – but in any case have fuelled the fears and speculations that resulted from the culture of secrecy which grew from the initial cover-ups.

For instance, from 1977 former German Chancellor Willy Brandt headed a commission of eminent retired politicians and economists who, in 1980, published their collective report titled *North-South – A Programme for Survival*, which puts forward a comprehensive strategy for food, aid, environment, trade, finance and monetary reform – as well as proposals for global negotiations to achieve these objectives.[29] As a solution to the widening economic gap between the wealthy Northern and the impoverished Southern hemispheres, these proposals could be considered the first attempt on the part of humanity to begin to express its essential oneness, reflecting not only the advice of the space people towards solving the problems of the world, as we shall see in later chapters, but the essence of all the world's spiritual teachings as well.

However, as we know, the economic and financial power in the world has long been in the hands of several hundred wealthy families and institutions, a situation which was exacerbated when the neo-conservative view of life became dominant through the electoral victories of Margaret Thatcher in the UK ("There is no such thing as society") in 1979 and Ronald Reagan in the USA ("The best minds are not in government; if any were, business would steal them away") in 1980. This resulted in economic interests and values shifting from being a function of society to becoming the measure of all things, reducing society to a battlefield where the forces of materiality have been trying to finish what they had started through the Nazis in World War II.

The notion that everything, including human behaviour, may be reduced to empirical data gave credence to the idea that mankind is only motivated by self-interest, which informed the theories of early neo-liberal economists Friedrich von Hayek and James M. Buchanan. Its adoption by the Clinton Administration in the US and Tony Blair's New Labour government in the UK, which was compellingly chronicled in the 3-part BBC documentary *The Trap – What Happened to Our Dream of Freedom?*[30], left government policy all but in name in the hands of corporations and financial powerhouses such as the IMF and the World Bank.

As a result, the proposals in the Brandt Commission report were shelved and the ills of the world – hunger, poverty, inequality and divisions – were met with ever higher doses of what caused them in the first place: competition, greed and limited self-interest, enslaving more and more people in poverty or underpaid McJobs and consumerism, all in the name of the 'free market'.

One of the few disclosure advocates who have made this connection is former Canadian Defence minister and vice prime minister Paul Hellyer, who instantly rose to fame within the circles of disclosure and exopolitics activists when he declared, in a speech at the Exopolitics Toronto Symposium in September 2005, that "UFOs are as real as the airplanes flying overhead" and that "the veil of secrecy must be lifted". His recent book *Light at the End of the Tunnel – A Survival Plan for the Human Species* is that rare voice of reason from one who combines a lifetime of public service and a keen insight into the needs of the time, with an open-minded view of a broader reality which alone will guarantee the survival of humanity on this planet. The author's description of himself as a practising Christian shows that he is one of the true, tolerant kind, whose inclusive views are based on a solid understanding of the essential message of all the world's Teachers: "My philosophy can be summed up in three words: The Golden Rule" – the injunction to treat others the way we ourselves want to be treated (see Appendix).

Injustice, whether economic, social, ecological, political, religious, or scientific, is indeed seen by Mr Hellyer as a major obstacle to salvaging the world. Thus it is that in one chapter he eloquently and movingly denounces the plight of the Palestinian people as he experiences the Israeli policy of oppression first-hand, and in another sums up all the compelling evidence of the authenticity of the Shroud of Turin that is ignored by debunkers, while also identifying the 'star' of Bethlehem as "one of God's spaceships". Not surprisingly, then, Mr Hellyer describes the old world order as a place "where a combination of greed and incompetence can doom billions of people to lives of misery and hopelessness".[31]

So, while it is the structures of the current world order that have steadily diminished the freedom and justice of individuals and nations over the last 30-odd years and driven the world community towards the precipice, with no lack of support from the far right the conspirators booked another success now that the letters NWO (for 'New World Order') alone are enough to frighten the wits out of conspiracy-prone people.[32] This, of course, begs the question what is 'new' about oppression, competition, greed and ignorance? A truly new world order would more likely be built on co-operation, sharing, justice, and freedom for all as an expression of the essential oneness of humanity, based on the value of the individual and a sense of community.

Much in keeping with these misunderstandings the United Nations Organisation has been denounced as a mere instrument to establish this not-so-'New World Order', in the hands of the terrifying 'Illuminati', which is the name by which the world elite seems to go in circles of the misinformed. Despite its alleged ultra-secretive and all-powerful rule of the world for thousands of years, conspiracy theorists seem to have outsmarted them, claiming to have unearthed a trail of documentary evidence implicating this elite group of power brokers in their nefarious efforts, if not in their 'true' form as shape-shifting 'reptilians'.

A little more scrutiny, however, reveals quite a different history that gives little reason for the massive fear that seems to have entire Internet communities in thrall. As the Dutch writer and philosopher Benjamin Adamah explains, the present-day use of the term 'Illuminati', which is Latin for 'Enlightened Ones', derives from the German *Illuminatenorden* ("Order of the Enlightened") that was founded in 1778 by Adam Weishaupt (1748-1830), a German philosopher and freemason who sought a more enlightened form of government outside the paradigm of nation-states. Adamah shows that Weishaupt's Order of the Enlightened only existed for about eight years, and began to dissolve after it had been made illegal in 1784 because they advocated more individual freedoms and opposed the political and social systems that existed before the French Revolution. Adamah goes on to show that about a hundred years afterwards some attempts were made to establish similar groups under the same name, which failed without exception. The name 'Illuminati' was then picked up by reactionaries and obscurantists as a red herring to incriminate the Jews in an alleged plot to rule the world, notably by John Robison in his book *Proofs of a Conspiracy against all the Religions and Governments of Europe* (1798) and the early 20th century *Protocols of the Elders of Zion*, which originated as a Russian forgery, and contributed to the world's passive on-looking when the Nazis hounded the Jews. [33]

To summarize then, the original Illuminati proposed a "kingship of philosophers" to replace the despot kings of their time – the historical equivalent in Europe of the unelected corporate interests that rule the world today. And according to the Ageless Wisdom teaching, the original "kingship of philosophers" was found in the civilizations of Atlantis, where the initiates and Masters of Wisdom of yore were the enlightened rulers of the masses, who were not yet gifted with individuality and possessed only embryonic mental capabilities. [34]

These Masters of Wisdom did indeed become a secret society when They withdrew to remote mountain and desert centres during the final destruction of the Atlantean continent some 98.000 years ago, and They were and still are the Enlightened Ones who, in every age, have sent a Teacher from their midst to inspire humanity to re-align itself with the Plan of Evolution. Likewise, the Freemasons, or Masonry in general, are the remnants of a group of disciples of the Masters of Wisdom who were in training in Atlantean times. [35] In other words, neither the real Enlightened Ones, nor the historical

Illuminati have anything to do with the sinister plans of their imaginary evil twins or indeed with attempts to control the world's wealth and resources.

One of the people who is regularly accused of having aligned herself with the nefarious efforts of the alleged 'Illuminati', especially by fundamentalist Christians, is Alice A. Bailey who, from 1919 to 1949, worked as the amanuensis for the Tibetan Master Djwhal Khul (DK), elaborating on the preparatory phase of the teachings as given through Mme Blavatsky. However, her all but forgotten book *Between War and Peace* should leave no doubt as to the intentions of either herself or the Elder Brothers of humanity. In it she defines the conflict between the Axis Powers and the Allied Nations of World War II as a fundamental spiritual struggle for the victory of the divine nature of man, contrasting the stated aims of Hitler and Mussolini with the Four Freedoms as pronounced by then-US president Franklin D. Roosevelt in the ten "Realities For Which We Fight".

Thus she compares the goal of the dark forces, "A vision of material good..." by forcing standardisation and regimentation upon the masses, with the vision of the forces of light as "a way of life which is based on true values and a fair distribution of the world's resources..." through "opportunity for all and the fostering of initiative..."[36]

Benjamin Creme defines the forces of materiality as the relatively few families, corporations and institutions who own the majority of the wealth of our planet. "Naturally they make every effort to hold on to the power that this gives them. So it has been throughout the ages on this Earth. It holds back the evolution of the planet."[37] Indeed, as a recent study by three complex systems theorists at the Swiss Federal Institute of Technology in Zurich shows, 43,000 transnational corporations can be traced to 147 corporate interests.[38] And although they may be more selfish or greedy than most of us, that does not necessarily make them 'shape-shifting reptilians'.

As with the so-called 'new' world order, then, the conspiracists have their labels seriously mixed up when it comes to identifying the progressive and reactionary forces in the world. There is nothing "enlightened" about wanting to rule the world and subjugate humanity, while the truly Enlightened Ones have always inspired and guided humanity towards greater understanding, compassion and freedom.

A truly new world order will be based on sharing, justice and co-operation for the greater good of all – to replace the current self-serving culture of grab-all-you-can greed and competition. The problem of economic injustice that results from such extreme concentration of wealth, which condems millions of men, women and children to living standards below that of the average domestic pet in the Western world (as well as in emerging economic powerhouses), is inextricably connected with the problems of pollution and climate change, and must therefore be tackled on a global scale through equal representation of the nations.

Despite its current imperfections, the logical platform for the world to work towards solutions to these problems is the United Nations Organisation, which is not a stepping stone towards a world government, but rather a world parliament, or in the words of Benjamin Creme, "a 'sounding board' for the exchange of all different, perhaps contradictory, ideas, and is essential to the free exchange of such ideas. It is the hope of humanity for a better and better ordered, peaceful, humane world."[39] But first, of course, it needs to be stripped of the Security Council which only serves the interests of the major military and economic powers that shy away from democratic control and public accountability in corporate-controlled institutions such as the World Bank and the IMF, and secretive conferences like the Bilderberg meetings.

However, investigative journalist Chip Berlet writes in *The New Internationalist* (the self-described 'First stop for global justice'): "Conspiracy theorists are correct about one thing: the *status quo* is not acceptable. They have accurately understood that there are inequalities of power and privilege in the world – and threats to the world itself – that need to be rectified. What conspiracy theorists lack is either the desire or ability to follow the basic rules of logic." Their selective perception, he adds, "allows conspiracy theorists to latch on to eccentric crumb-sized claims while ignoring mountains of easily documented evidence."[40]

Moreover, while it may be true that the elites of the world are conspiring in seclusion to secure their power, current developments such as the 'Arab Spring', the student movements in various countries, and the worldwide 'Occupy' movement show that they are working against the tide. Benjamin Creme's Master sees these recent popular uprisings in the Arab world and in debt-ridden Western nations as "the voice of the new time, the time of justice and sharing, freedom and love. It is the voice of the people, and the people have awakened to their unity and power. For the old despots, the writing is on the wall."[41]

During his last reported visit to a Venusian mother ship, in August 1954, George Adamski was made aware of the precursor to this development when Orthon told him: "It has also been foretold that when the time cometh, the dark races of the world will rise up and demand the right to equal respect and the lot of free men so long denied them by you of lighter skins." In a clear reference to the post-war wave of de-colonization and the nascent civil rights movement in the US, he added: "Is not this prophecy, too, being fulfilled in these very days on Earth?"[42]

Psychologically, conspiracy-thinking might be considered an understandable response to feeling excluded when a person with less than average self-confidence learns that there are aspects to life which they feel they are being kept in the dark about by a small group of others who are in the know because of their position of socio-economic or else of spiritual privilege. At the same time it could be seen to some extent as an act of disobedience against authorities that are fast losing credibility, evincing the expression of an increased sense of individuality that the cosmic energies of Pisces are said to have bestowed on humanity[43] during the age whose end is now marked by the growing visibility of the Space Brothers in support of the reappearance of the Elder Brothers of humanity.

Notes

1 Richard Dawkins (2007), *The Enemies of Reason*, episode 2: 'The Irrational Health Service'. Channel Four TV (UK), 20 August.
2 Carl Sagan (1997), *The Demon-Haunted World*, pp.196-97
3 The Tibetan Master Djwhal Khul, in Alice A. Bailey (1944), *Discipleship in the New Age, Vol.I*, 11th printing, 1985, p.viii
4 Ibidem, p.91

Life, a universal principle

5 Benjamin Creme (2010), public lecture in Nagoya, Japan, 18 May.
6 Sylvia Cranston (1993), *HPB – The Extraordinary Life and Influence of Helena Blavatsky, Founder of the Modern Theosophical Movement*, p.xx
7 Ibid., p.xvii
8 Helena P. Blavatsky (1890), 'The Dual Aspect of Wisdom'. *Lucifer*, Vol. VII, No.37, 15 September, pp.1-9. Available at <www.theosociety.org/pasadena/hpb-sio/sio-dual.htm>
9 Benjamin Creme's Master (1982), 'A new era dawns', *Share International* magazine, Vol.1, No.7, July, p.2
10 Benjamin Creme (1979), *The Reappearance of the Christ and the Masters of Wisdom*, p.222

11 See for instance: BBC News (2011), 'Buried city revealed by satellite'. [online] 25 May. Available at <www.bbc.co.uk/news/world-13518143> [Accessed 26 May 2011]

Cover-ups, conspiracies and speculation
12 Pen name of Aladino Felix. It seems the ridicule that befell Mr Felix led him to eventually recant his claims.
13 Alberto Perego (1963), *L'aviazione di altri pianeti opera tra noi: rapporto agli italiani: 1943-1963*, p.63
14 Gerard Aartsen (2010), *George Adamski – A Herald for the Space Brothers*, pp.52-54
15 George Adamski (1955a), *Many Mansions*, 1974 reprint, pp.5-6
16 Adamski (1955), *Inside the Space Ships*, p.99
17 Wilbert B. Smith, letter dated 23 February 1959, as quoted in Ronald Caswell (1967), 'In Defence of Wilbert Smith', *UFO Contact*, IGAP Journal Vol.2, No.8, December, p.203
18 Creme (2010), *The Gathering of the Forces of Light – UFOs and their Spiritual Mission*, p.48
19 Laurent Basset (dir.; 2002), *The Secret – Evidence We Are Not Alone.*
20 'Cutler-Twining Memo', 14 July 1954. Source: Laurent Basset (dir.; 2002), op cit. The authenticity of the MJ-12 documents has been confirmed by Benjamin Creme in a private communication between one of his London associates and a US co-worker.
21 'Air Force Order on "Saucers" Cited – Pamphlet by the Inspector General Called Objects a "Serious Business"'. *New York Times*, [online] 28 February 1960. Available at: <www.theufochronicles.com/2009/09/former-cia-director-adm-rh.html> [Accessed 12 October 2012]
22 Adamski (1957-58), *Cosmic Science for the Promotion of Cosmic Principles and Truths*, Part 3, Question #57
23 Gordon W. Creighton (1963), 'The Italian Scene – Part 3: Bruno Ghibaudi's contact claim'. *Flying Saucer Review* Vol.9, No.3, May-June, p.18
24 Wilbert B. Smith (n.d.), 'Official Reticence', *Flying Saucer Review*, Vol.6, No.3, 1960, as quoted in Timothy Good (1988), *Above Top Secret*, p.198
25 Lou Zinsstag & Timothy Good (1983), *George Adamski – The Untold Story*, p.44
26 Creme (2010), op cit, p.48
27 Ibid., p.49
28 Ibid., p.50

The *new* world order?
29 Willy Brandt (ed.; 1980), *North-South – A Programme for Survival*
30 Adam Curtis (dir.; 2007), *The Trap – What Happened to Our Dream of Freedom?*, Part 2: 'The Lonely Robot'

31 Paul Hellyer (2010), *Light at the End of the Tunnel. A Survival Plan for the Human Species*, p.211

32 Wikipedia, 'New World Order (conspiracy theory) – History of the term'. Available at <en.wikipedia.org/wiki/New_World_Order_(conspiracy_theory)#History_of_the_term> [Accessed 31 March 2011]

33 Benjamin Adamah (2008), "De Illuminati bestaan niet" (The Illuminati do not exist). Lecture for Delft University of Technology Studium Generale, [online] 3 November. Available at <collegerama.tudelft.nl/mediasite/Viewer/?peid=1da12dee770a42f89000d42125d02cdf1d>

34 Bailey (1957), *The Externalization of the Hierarchy*, pp.121-124.

35 Bailey (1934), *A Treatise on White Magic*, 14th printing, 1979, pp.398-99

36 Bailey (1942), *Between War and Peace*, pp.62-64

37 Creme (2010), op cit, p.46

38 Andy Coghlan and Debora MacKenzie (2011), 'Revealed – the capitalist network that runs the world'. *New Scientist* magazine No.2835, [online] 22 October, pp.8-9. Available at <www.newscientist.com/article/mg21228354.500-revealed--the-capitalist-network-that-runs-the-world.html> [Accessed 24 October 2011]

39 Creme (ed.; 2010a),'Questions and Answers', *Share International* magazine Vol.29, No.9, November, p.23

40 Chip Berlet (2007), 'Siren Song – Conspiracy!'. *The New Internationalist*, issue 405 [online], October. Available at <www.newint.org/features/2007/10/01/paranoia/> [Accessed 1 August 2011]

41 Benjamin Creme's Master (2011), 'The voice of the people is heard'. *Share International*, Vol.30, No.2, March, p.3

42 Adamski (1955), op cit, p.241

43 Bailey (1951), *A Treatise on the Seven Rays, Volume III – Esoteric Astrology*, 10th printing 1975, pp.472-73

3. Meanwhile, in reality

As we have seen, the conspiracies that many fear are mostly in people's imagination as a result of the initial cover-up of the extraterrestrial presence, and are only partly based in the age-old reality of powers-that-be who protect their own limited self-interests, instead of serving the needs of the people.

More and more, though, these Earth-spun conspiracies have been conflated with the alleged 'alien' threat that arose from the attempts to keep the public in the dark about the reality and origin of the UFOs and the contacts between the visitors from space and the authorities which took place in the second half of the 20th century. As a result, many people are now convinced that, while there may be benevolent visitors, quite a few are here to 'abduct' people for alle manner of atrocities, with a view to subjecting people, which doesn't make much sense if they have been coming here for at least decades, but more likely millennia. If they were serious about conquering the planet or humanity, "with their superior knowledge", as Adamski calls it, "they could have conquered the world long ago."[1]

One fact that is consistently ignored when people take for granted the validity of 'alien abduction' claims, is that none of the early contactees ever spoke of having been abducted by the visitors from space. Strikingly, stories about 'abductions' only began to appear *after* covert government agents had begun their defamation and disinformation campaign against the contactees of the 1950s, and especially against George Adamski who, as the most popular and well-known among them, was reaching a world-wide audience and who was the first individual to be met with organized opposition and sabotage.[2]

Asked about the intentions of the space visitors, Adamski once said: "We all know the power they have tapped would make our largest bombs look like dud firecrackers on the 4th of July. Do not these facts adequately answer questions regarding their hostility? To the best of my knowledge, there have been no proven incidents of hostility from space travelers towards the people of Earth. As for the reported monsters, have you ever seen one of our own jet pilots in full regalia for high altitude flight? I think you will find reports of 'monsters' were the result of a combination of intense fear caused by the strangeness and nearness of the space craft, and the appearance of an unfamiliar uniform."[3]

Is there then no truth in any of the reports from people who claim to have been beamed up, experimented on, given implants et cetera? According to Benjamin Creme, "All of this is totally untrue. There is not a single instance of such happenings. All of these stories are the result either of the fevered astral imagination of people who want to feel these things and do so in an astral sense, which they then describe to others and so build up a climate; or work of certain negative forces in the world whose aim it is to keep from the public the reality of the extraterrestrial connection of this planet..."[4] Similarly, in answer to a request to indicate which books by other authors were genuine, Adamski once said: "This would not be a wise thing to do, because I am sure many of those who have written believe their experiences to be genuine. To them they are real ... but so are dreams to the dreamer. And it is unfortunate that much of the literature written about contacts falls into this category."[5]

Dr Steven Greer, founder of The Disclosure Project, wrote in 2006 that his organization has found "a multi-decade pattern of hoaxed UFO/ET related events that are clustered around pseudo-contact experiences (also known as abductions), mutilations, vivisections and the like. Numerous, corroborative military and shadowy para-governmental witnesses have testified to actually conducting abductions and mutilations for their psychological warfare value. One such witness, an Army Ranger involved with special ops stated to me: 'You have no idea how many people – including prominent military and political figures – we have abducted and terrified so that they will learn to hate the ET presence and support conflict with them…' "[6]

Creme's assertion that this is a "climate" that was created by fear and ignorance is supported in poll results quoted by the late Major Hans C. Petersen, Adamski's associate in Denmark, who said that "reported instances of abductions outside the American Continent – Canada, the US, Central and South America – until lately, did not primarily exist. Yet, about the time after the last poll, where 10 million Americans indicated their belief in being abducted, then suddenly claimed abductions began sprouting up elsewhere. So today, it can be said that 98% of all claimed abductions took place on the American continent, while the last 2% were found elsewhere – typically England and Germany."[7]

In his 1993 article 'Are they coming for us?' astrophysicist and cosmologist Dr Carl Sagan, who himself seems to have rejected an extraterrestrial explanation for the UFO phenomenon, pointed out: "Based upon a Roper Poll of American adults specially commissioned by those who accept the alien abduction story at face value, the poll's sponsors concluded that 2 per cent of all Americans (believe themselves to) have been abducted, many repeatedly by beings from other worlds. *If* aliens are not partial to Americans, the number for the whole planet would be more than 100 million people. This means an abduction every few seconds. It's surprising that more of the neighbors haven't noticed." Sagan pointedly adds: "Why should beings so advanced in physics and engineering – crossing vast interstellar distances – be so backward when it comes to biology?"[8]

Indeed, as Benjamin Creme says: "It is complete nonsense that [the Space Brothers] should carry out genetic or sexual experimentation on people from this planet when they have a technology which is several thousand years ahead of anything that we could think of today. It is stupid, a deliberate way of attacking the concept of wise and superior, spiritually oriented people."[9] Elsewhere he adds: "[T]here are agencies, particularly in the USA, whose job for many years has been to denigrate the Space Brothers. They are government agencies but not necessarily known to the officials of the administration... They are experts in their particular line of work, which is to do with corrupting human minds..."[10]

His statements are corroborated by Italian contactee Paolo di Girolamo, who was one of the people involved in the Italian Amicizia (Friendship) Case, and who said in his book *Noi e Loro* ('Us and Them'): "The governments of our world, especially the American, have all the interest in giving the public a negative view of the extraterrestrials, who appear to be motivated, instead, by positive intentions."[11] The author says we are using the technology which they gave us, and large sums of money, to 'protect' and 'defend' our planet from their nonexistent hostility. The fact that conspiracy theorists fail to see that the large 'black' budgets which they suspect or claim to have documented may well be used to stage drug- or hypnosis induced 'abductions', cattle mutilations, et cetera, rather than a secret base on Mars, indicates a blind spot similar to that which troubles most scientists when it comes to acknowledging the reality of extraterrestrial space craft.

Reputable eye-witnesses

Another significant factor that is generally overlooked in this debate is the fact that whenever dignitaries or officials – historical or contemporary – *do* go on the record about their personal experiences, they are unanimously favourable in the description of their contacts. It should be noted here that these are mostly people who have everything to lose in terms of public credibility by coming out with their stories, and who would be acting against their own interests if they belonged to the elite who benefit from a negative perception of extraterrestrials.

In addition to the current spate of government and military officials who have acknowledged their knowledge of or experiences with extraterrestrial craft and their capabilities, several high profile cases have recently come to light in which space people from other planets seem to have contacted high-ranking individuals on Earth.

One such encounter involved Kirsan Ilyumzhinov, President of the southern Russian state of Kalmykia, who says he met with extraterrestrial visitors at his Moscow apartment on 18 September 1997, and spent hours on board their spaceship. In an interview with journalist Vladimir Pozner on Russia's main Channel One Mr Ilyumzhinov explained that he heard his balcony door being opened and someone calling him. When he went over to take a look he was invited into the space craft and given a tour. The president was just being brought home by his extraterrestrial hosts when his driver, a government minister, and his assistant were about to launch a full-scale search upon finding the apartment empty in the morning.

Mr Ilyumzhinov, who has also been the head of the world chess federation FIDE since 1995, seemed to indicate that he communicated with the space visitors through telepathy when he said: "I am often asked which language I used to talk to them. Perhaps it was on a level of the exchange of ideas."

What follows is a transcript of part of the interview, which was aired on 26 April 2010: "It was a Saturday evening in September 1997. I was in the terrace of my apartment, in Leontiefski Lane here in Moscow, and I had to leave for Kalmykia soon. That evening, I read a book, watched television, and I took a rest. I fell asleep and I had the feeling that someone called me through the balcony door, which was open.

"When I got up I saw a sort of semi-translucent moon. I got into this tube and I saw people in yellow space suits. (...) They took me on a visit to their ship, where they said: *'We need to take samples elsewhere on the planet.'* Then there was a dialogue: *'Why don't you go live on television channels to say that you're here?' 'Watch, communicate with us.'* They told me: *'[The world] is not ready to meet us.'* Afterwards they took me back home.

"I would probably not have believed it myself, if there hadn't been three witnesses – my driver, a minister and my assistant, who arrived in the morning and found that I was not there. Things were in their place, the balcony door was open (my apartment is on the top floor). They looked around and began to call friends... Then they sat in the kitchen, looking for someone to call or whom to contact because my [mobile] phone and everything was there; the apartment was locked but they had their own key to the apartment. Then they saw me come out of the bedroom and they followed me into the kitchen. They looked at me and (...) asked me: *'Where were you?'* I told them, as if it was normal, *'Well, I have been flying. I was in a UFO.'* They were upset and added: *'We are serious.'*

"So I sat down and put myself to think logically. All the time that they were there, almost an hour, I was not in my apartment. One of them was in the lobby, so I could not have passed through there, while I came out of the room that has a bay window which overlooks the open balcony. So for several months, they remained in shock over this.

"Well, understandably so, because if it had not been me, I would not have believed it. On the other hand, when I look back and talk about it with them again, I still have trouble believing it myself."[12]

While many media referred to Mr Ilyumzhinov's experience as an "abduction", he himself never used that word. In fact, in an interview on British TV, he said about his extraterrestrial hosts: "They are people like us. They have the same mind, the same vision. I talked with them, I understand that we are not alone in this whole world [universe]. We are not unique."[13]

It was not the first time that Mr Ilyumzhinov had spoken out about his contacts with extraterrestrials, as he had already talked about his experience on Radio Svoboda on 22 July 2002. However, his candid interview on prime-time television in 2007 prompted an MP of the Liberal Democrat Party to call on Russian President Medvedev to investigate if Mr Ilyumzhinov had perchance disclosed state secrets. In a letter to the Kremlin, Mr Andrei Lebedev, a member of the parliament's Security Committee, wrote: "I ask you to say if the head of Kalmykia has made an official report to the Russian presidency about his contacts with representatives of an alien civilization. Is there an established procedure of informing about such contacts by high-ranking people who have access to secret information like Ilyumzhinov? And did he in the course of his seemingly innocent conversation disclose secret information?"

Unruffled, Mr Ilyumzhinov, who was the governor of the

Buddhist republic of Kalmykia from 1993 until 2010, responded: "Pozner asked. I replied. If someone, including the respected Duma Deputy Andrei Lebedev, has any more questions, I am ready to meet and discuss any topic."[14]

A similar report, albeit by proxy, of a world leader having met with the space people involves the late US President Dwight Eisenhower. In a statement released on 8 May 2010 former US State Representative for New Hampshire Henry W. McElroy Jr said: "We know that highly advanced knowledge and information can assist human beings in solving various problems both in our current time and in the future."

Mr McElroy had his personal testimony about a document that he saw while he served on the State Federal Relations and Veterans Affairs Committee, filmed and published on YouTube: "The document I saw was an official brief to President Eisenhower... This brief was pervaded with a sense of hope, and it informed President Eisenhower of the continued presence of extraterrestrial beings here in the United States of America.

"The tone of the brief indicated to me that there was no need for concern, since these visitors were in no way causing any harm or had any intentions whatsoever of causing any disruption then or in the future. Because of his optimism in his farewell address in 1961, I personally believe that Eisenhower did indeed meet with these extraterrestrial, off-world astronauts."

McElroy went on to thank former astronauts as well as several former army, navy and government officials, "who deserve the admiration of the American people for sharing their accounts publicly, in an effort to elevate our knowledge to a higher understanding of our existence."[15] Interestingly, ufologists have long claimed that President Eisenhower met with the space visitors at Edwards Air Force Base in California, in February 1954, and again in 1955.

Significantly, in this context, in his press conference with the ministers of Detroit in September 1955, George Adamski referred to an article in *The Examiner*[16], which stated that during the Geneva Conference in July 1955 between US President Dwight D. Eisenhower, British Prime Minister Anthony Eden, premier Nikolai A. Bulganin of the Soviet Union, and French Prime Minister Edgar Fauré, "the [Four] Powers would discuss conditions in reference to the people – they did not say spaceships, they referred to people – of other worlds. As much as to say, *they are here!*"[17]

The "sense of hope" as reported by Henry McElroy is reflected not only in the information coming from early contactees such as George Adamski and Wilbert Smith that, if the UFOs were here to colonize or conquer, with their superior technology they could have done so centuries ago. It also reverberates in the testimonies of army officials such as Robert Salas, who have commented that while the presence of UFOs over nuclear arms silos may have disarmed them, they clearly did not intend to cause any damage, as described in Chapter 1.

In confirmation of the Eisenhower brief, one of the Majestic-12 documents (see Chapter 2) that were leaked to US researcher Tim S. Cooper starting in 1994 states: "As to purpose and modus operandi, we are not certain, but it is clear, that if these visitors had conquest in mind, it would not be difficult for them, given their ability to penetrate our airspace at will, and their ability to jam radio, telephone, television and teletype transmissions, let alone power grids."[18]

The Vatican connection

In a somewhat philosophical commentary for *The Independent* newspaper, UK space scientist Dr David Whitehouse recently assessed the possible stance of the different religions on intelligent extraterrestrial beings, saying: "Islam will welcome them. The Koran actually mentions life from outer space, and some Muslims have said it is the height of conceit to suppose that God created the vastness of the universe just for us to enjoy when we will never see the vast majority of it". In his description of the Buddhist and Hindu response to extraterrestrials, with their philosophy of oneness and unity, Dr Whitehouse goes so far as to say, "they will have no problem accepting them as part of a cosmic brotherhood of consciousness".

Dr Whitehouse thinks that Christianity might find it hardest to adapt to the 'new' reality if science were to discover life outside our own planet: "One day we may converse with an alien. A future Pope and it may discuss questions of faith. But before that takes place, the search itself forces us to finally confront uncomfortable questions about our beliefs. If we are made 'in the image and likeness of God', are creatures from the depths of space and who bear us no biological relationship, also made in his image?"[19]

In the same article, however, Dr Whitehouse also quotes a statement made by the director of the astronomical Vatican Observatory José Gabriel Funes in an interview for the Italian newspaper L'Osservatore Romano in 2008, that "God could have created intelligent life in other parts of the Universe and they could even be our brothers", a statement that swiftly spread around the world.

The connection between the Vatican and UFOs first became public in the English newspaper The Sun and later on 23 July 1985 in a US newspaper. It was revealed that during the 1960s Pope John XXIII, also known as the "good Pope", to whom thousands of miracles and healings are ascribed all over the world, had encounters with extraterrestrial beings.

A well-documented encounter took place one evening in

July 1961 at the Pope's summer residence of Castel Gandolfo, Italy. While in the garden, the Pope and one of his assistants saw an unusual craft in the sky: "It was oval and had blue and amber flashing lights. The craft seemed to fly over our heads for a few minutes and then landed over the grass on the south end of the garden. A strange being came out of the craft, he looked human, except that he was surrounded by a golden light and had pointed ears. The Pope and I kneeled down. We didn't know what we were witnessing. But we knew that it was not from this world, so it should have been a celestial event. The Holy Father stood up and walked towards the being. The two of them spent 15 to 20 minutes together. It seemed they talked intensely. They did not call me, so I remained where I was and could not hear anything of the conversation. The being turned around and walked towards the craft and left rightaway. The Pontiff came towards me and told me: 'The sons of God are everywhere. Sometimes we have difficulties in recognizing our own brothers'."

At the time this report did not have much impact but in 2007 it was discussed again at the UFO Expert Congress in Peru by the Bishop of the Ecumenical Catholic Church of Jesus Christ, Higinio Alas, who in a phone interview said: "When we believe in the reality that God the Father stamped his seal on the whole Universe, His seal of life, there has to be life in other galaxies and planets". The story was subsequently picked up by Mexican UFO researcher Jaime Maussan in his TV programme *Tercer Milenio*.[20]

A description in the book *Le profezie di Papa Giovanni* ('The prophecies of Pope John'; 1976) by Pier Carpi of an event that occurred in 1935 gains in significance in light of this close encounter between the Pope and a space visitor. In an initiation ritual performed in a Rosicrucian temple, one of the brothers began to speak in a voice not his own. The Lord Chancellor of the order transcribed everything the brother said: "The lights of heaven will be red, blue and green. And they will be fast. Someone that comes from far away wants to meet us, the Son of Earth. And already there have been encounters. But the ones who really saw them, had remained silent". The brother was Angelo Roncalli, then bishop of Bergamo, Italy, who would later become Pope under the name of John XXIII.[21]

As an interesting side note, during his last lecture tour of Europe, George Adamski met with Pope John XXIII on 31 May 1963. According to Lou Zinsstag, who accompanied him on much of his tour of Europe, Adamski was given access to the Pope's residence through a small doorway in one of the high wooden entrance gates to the left of the Dome of St Peter's, away from the Swiss Guards. He later told Mrs Zinsstag that he had indeed been received by the Pope, who said to him: "I have been expecting you." He also handed the Pope a sealed message which he had received earlier from a Space Brother in Copenhagen. In return, the Pope presented Adamski with a new Ecumenical Council medallion, which would only go on sale after the demise of Pope John XXIII, two days later.[22]

One more example of a public figure to make statements about the nature of the space visitors is former astronaut Dr Edgar Mitchell. As a rigorously trained scientist and the sixth man to walk on the moon, Dr Mitchell brings to bear not only his reputation, but also his professional experience when he says in a 2008 radio interview in the UK: "There's life throughout the Universe, we're not alone in the Universe at all. (…) I know for sure we're not alone in the universe. (…) I happen to be privileged enough to be in on the fact that we have been visited on this planet and the UFO phenomenon is real, although it's been covered up by governments for quite a long time."

Although Dr Mitchell says there is more nonsense going around about the nature of UFOs than actual knowledge, the fact that "a number of contacts are real and on-going is pretty well known to those of us who have been briefed and been close to the subject matter". As to the intent of the extraterrestrial visitors, Dr Mitchell unambiguously reassured both the host and his listeners: "No, no, it's not hostile. It's pretty obvious that if it had been hostile we would have been gone by now. (...) We have no defence, if that is what their real intent was."[23]

Spiritual reality check

These are just some instances of reputable first-hand witnesses from different parts of the world and from various stations in life who testify to the singularly benign intentions of the space people they have met or know about. Thus, we now not only have the early contactees or Benjamin Creme, but also several high-profile dignitaries and officials who insist that the visitors from space are not here for selfish purposes.

Having advanced to the point where they arguably understand more of Life and its manifestations in the various kingdoms of nature than we do, the space people of necessity know more about us than we do ourselves, and therefore simply have no need to carry out any of the atrocities that have been attributed to them as a result of the secrecy that stoked up these ugly, one would almost say anthropomorphic, inferences. As Adamski explained: "[W]e must know ourselves before we can recognize our brothers from other worlds. For they differ from us only in understanding."[24]

Self-knowledge seems to be a prerequisite for advancement and growth in consciousness. Not for nothing do all the major Teachings of the ages exhort us to learn about ourselves, our true nature, if we are to progress on the path of evolution, such as in the adage of the Delphic Oracle: "Man, know thyself!" Similarly, according to the apocryphal Gospel of Thomas, Jesus said: "When you know yourselves, then you will be known, and you will understand that you are children of the living Father."[25] Or, as H.P. Blavatsky explains: "…Esoteric Philosophy solved, ages ago, the problem of what man *was*, *is* and *will be*; his origin, life-cycle (…) and his final absorption into the Source from which he started."[26] Those who are ahead of us on the path of evolution back to the Source understand more of our essence than average humanity, and are therefore better able to express the human condition in their work – be they artists, writers, composers, scientists, philosophers or teachers.[27]

This, then, gives ample evidence in support of the claims by Benjamin Creme, whose work builds on the groundwork that was laid by H.P. Blavatsky (HPB) and the elaborations on that in the books by Alice A. Bailey, that authentic contacts with the space people are always of a positive nature, in support of humanity's awakening from its cosmic slumber as it is ready to rejoin the cosmic brotherhood of consciousness that it lost sight of when, in Atlantean times, mankind began to stray from the path that is laid out in the Plan of Evolution for this planet. If nothing else, the many predictions of a "quantum leap" in consciousness, the "opening of interdimensional portals", the "ascension" of humanity, or simply a "breakthrough" in spiritual awareness are different ways, more or less informed, to express the fact that the world's mind-belt is saturated with the notion that the human race is ready to face the spiritual realities of life once again, which have forever been reiterated in the teachings of terrestrial and extraterrestrial origin – that all life is inter-connected (hence the need for harmlessness in our relations), and that we need to find a way to put this realization into practice if we are to prevent the ultimate destruction of ourselves and this planet. In short, humanity has to take responsibility for its part in the Plan.

An interesting illustration of the fact that the human kingdom is growing in consciousness comes from two examples of 'supernatural' occurrences, almost a century apart. The first is taken from *The Theosophist*, edited by HPB, and shows that the Western world was still getting to grips with the idea of life after death only 130 years ago. In the July 1880 issue, HPB's sister Vera Zelihovski recounts the story of a widow in her hometown Tiflis (Tiblisi), whose son had been accidentally killed in an incident at a local inn. The perpetrators had hidden the body in a stack of hay, but before they could dispose of it the following night the ghost of the young man, or the "astral double", had guided his mother to the place where his physical body was hidden.[28]

The second is a story which was said to have first been found in a secret report that was smuggled out of the Soviet Union by a defecting scientist and was picked up by *Weekly World News* in its edition of 22 October 1985. According to the report three Soviet cosmonauts witnessed the most awe-inspiring spectacle on their 155th day aboard the Salyut 7 space station in July 1985. What they saw was a band of glowing angels with wings as large as jumbo jets, their faces round with cherubic smiles. Twelve days later the figures were also seen by six other Soviet scientists, including cosmonaut Svetlana Savitskaya. "They were smiling," she said, "as though they shared in a glorious secret." Asked about the nature of this phenomenon, Benjamin Creme's Master elucidated in *Share International* magazine that it was a vision projected in astral matter by the Master Jesus. "Its purpose was to bring to their minds the idea of higher worlds and meaning..."[29]

With the expansion of consciousness the world has got

steadily smaller. As Benjamin Creme says, "People know what is going on in the world. They know people are starving to death. People in big rich nations like America and Europe know people are dying. We used to see them dying on our television screens but that is no longer shown because we would turn off and so miss the commercials. Nevertheless, people are dying from starvation all the time. Five million children die each year from diseases related to malnutrition. This should not be happening. We have the answer to all these illnesses. There is a surplus of food in the world of 12 per cent per capita. It is simply not distributed. The answer to the economic problem is the redistribution of the resources of the world. This would create universal justice and, therefore, peace. It is the only way to peace."[30]

Humanity's real challenge, then, is not with nefarious 'aliens' or runaway robber barons from some fantastical 'break-away civilization', hiding here or elsewhere in our solar system, but with our own ignorance and fear, and our separativeness and greed as a result – ignorance of our spiritual nature, or rather, the spiritual nature of life, and the fear that has been actively, and often criminally, engendered by the clandestine efforts of government operatives in the service of robber barons at home – reinforced by 'Hollywood' and by everyone who perpetuates, against their better knowledge, the inaccurate and unjust portrayals of the interplanetary Helpers of humanity.

Because the governments of the world have gone to such great lengths to keep their populace in the dark about the true nature of the visitors from space, fear-based speculation has replaced proper reasoning and research. And because economic and military interests conspired to portray the space people in their own image – i.e. power-hungry, self-serving and harmful – conspiracy theories have replaced the message of hope that the original contactees brought to the world, in accordance with the actual purpose of their visits.

In all this we should remember that it is not important if one believes Benjamin Creme's claims that he is in constant telepathic contact with one of the Masters of Wisdom who gives him unique insights that are not otherwise available. Neither do we have to take it on Creme's 'authority' that the extraterrestrial presence on Earth is nothing to be feared, but rather an unqualified blessing. For, as should now be clear, the argument for the benign nature of the extraterrestrial visitors is supported not only by the legacy of the Ageless Wisdom teaching, which tells us about the existence on our own planet of people who have evolved beyond the strictly human state – the Masters of Wisdom, as witnessed in the lives and work of the historical Teachers of humanity and many of their disciples before Benjamin Creme[31], but also by the testimonies of the early contactees, and their subsequent debunking by the authorities. In addition we have the testimonies of later contactees, direct or by proxy, some of whom are officials and dignitaries from different parts of the world, different generations, and different walks of life.

Combined with the simple facts about the actual origins of the conspiracy theories as documented in the previous chapter, this amounts to a bulwark of facts and experiences that not only make sense and mutually support each other, but also contain an inner logic and build on the existing wisdom, knowledge and experience that constitute the shared legacy of the human race.

Taken together these solidly refute the notion of a 'predatory' universe that underlies the belief in nefarious 'alien' races which has been promoted to disqualify the message of hope as given through the original contactees.

Notes

1 George Adamski (1957-58), *Cosmic Science for the promotion of Cosmic Principles and Truths*, Series 1, Part No.3, Question #58

2 See Gerard Aartsen (2010), *George Adamski – A Herald for the Space Brothers*, Chapter 3, the section 'The opposition', pp.50-55

3 Adamski (1957-58), op cit, Part No.1, Question 20

4 Benjamin Creme (2001), *The Great Approach – New Light and Life for Humanity*, p.131

5 Adamski (1957-58), op cit, Part 5, Question #88

6 Steven Greer (2006), 'Exopolitics or Xenopolitics'. The Disclosure Project, [online] 2 May. Available at <www.disclosureproject.org/docs/pdf/ExopoliticsOrXenopolitics.pdf> [Accessed 10 July 2011]

7 Hans C. Peterson (n.d.), 'In Defence of the Abductees' (Denmark, Jelling: IGAPE-RCN). As quoted in Fred Steckling (n.d.), 'UFO Abductions and their validity'. Available at <www.adamskifoundation.com/html/News2.htm>

8 Carl Sagan (1993), 'Are they coming for us?'. *Parade Magazine*, March. As quoted in Fred Steckling, op cit

9 Creme (2010), *The Gathering of the Forces of Light – UFOs and their Spiritual Mission*, p.49

10 Ibidem, p.48

11 Paolo di Girolamo (2009), *Noi e Loro*, p.202

Reputable eye-witnesses

12 Translated from the French transcription at <lestempspresents.over-blog.com/article-abduction-d-un-gouverneur-russe-50672828.html> [Accessed 8 May 2011]

13 Available at <www.youtube.com/watch?v=ufCqRa5KZyk> [Accessed 12 September 2011]. Also referenced in Antonio Huneeus (2010), 'Russian-style Exopolitics – Kirsan Ilyumzhinov's alien abduction'. Open Minds TV [online] 16 June. Available at <www.openminds.tv/russian-exopolitics/> [Accessed 17 July 2011]

14 Tony Halpin (2010), 'Were Russian secrets shared with 'space alien' visitors?'. *The Times* [online] 7 May. Available at <www.timesonline.co.uk/tol/news/world/europe/article7118769.ece> [Accessed 16 June 2011]

15 'Former Legislator Makes Statement on Un-Released Eisenhower Brief' Available at <www.youtube.com/watch?v=mrK2YgfjnHo> See also: 'Behind the Story and How it Began', available at <brieftoeisenhower.wordpress.com/2010/05/21/behind-the-story-and-how-it-began/>

16 Given that Adamski lived in southern California, his reference was most likely to the Los Angeles *Examiner* (published from 1903 to 1962).

17 Adamski (1955a), *Many Mansions*, 1983 reprint, p.8.

18 'Majestic Twelve Project – Annual Report', Summer 1952 (?) Available at <www.majesticdocuments.com/pdf/mj12_fifthannualreport.pdf>

The Vatican connection

19 David Whitehouse (2010), 'Is anybody out there – with a soul?'. *The Independent* [online], 3 November. Available at <www.independent.co.uk/opinion/faith/is-anybody-out-there-ndash-with-a-soul-2123442.html> [Accessed 1 August 2011]

20 *Share International* (2010), 'Pope John XXIII and UFOs'. Vol.29, No.6, July/August, p.12. (*Tercer Milenio* segment available at: <www.youtube.com/watch?v=rRC1Uqwac-8>.

21 Pier Carpi (1976), *Le Profezie di Papa Giovanni*, p.154

22 Lou Zinsstag and Timothy Good (1983), *George Adamski – The Untold Story*, pp.61-63

23 Interview with Dr Edgar Mitchell in Nick Margerrison (2008), Kerrang! Radio, UK, 23 July. Available at <www.youtube.com/watch?v=RhNdxdveK7c>

Spiritual reality check

24 Adamski (1957-58), op cit, Part No.4, Question #69

25 Elaine H. Pagels and Helmut Koester (1992), 'From Jesus to Christ – the story of the storytellers: The Gospel of Thomas'. In Robert J. Miller (ed.; 1995), *The Complete Gospels*. Article available at <www.liberatedthinking.com/data/Library/Christianity/Gospels/thomas.htm> [Accessed 2 August 2011]

26 H.P. Blavatsky (1888), *The Secret Doctrine,* 6th Adyar edition, 1971, vol.2, p.361

27 See e.g. Alice A. Bailey (1922), *Initiation, Human and Solar* or Benjamin Creme (1995), *The Ageless Wisdom Teaching – An Introduction to Humanity's Spiritual Legacy*

28 V.P. Zelihovsky (1880), 'A Spectre Guide'. In H.P. Blavatsky (ed; 1880), *The Theosophist*, Vol.I, No.10, July; centenary re-issue (USA, Mecosta, MI: Wizards Bookshelf, 1980), pp.245-46

29 Creme (ed.; 1986), *Share International* magazine Vol.4, No.3, March, p.20. The story was also discussed on the American TV programme *Praise the Lord* (Trinity Broadcasting Network, 29 May 1986; available at <www.itbn.org/index/detail/lib/Networks/sublib/TBN/ec/BwMDltMjoNfy02GuwND-iahAZNOmDoK1>

30 Creme (2010a), 'Questions and Answers', *Share International* magazine Vol.29, No.8, October, p.22

31 Aartsen (2008), *Our Elder Brothers Return – A History in Books*, published online at <www.biblioteca-ga.info>

Photograph of an extraterrestrial pilot. First published in Alberto Perego, *L'aviazione di altri pianeti opera tra noi: rapporto agli italiani: 1943-1963* (Rome, 1963)

4. From space in friendship

"Let's look at the photographs of a real extraterrestrial pilot (taken in Italy in 1957 [pages 54 and 57])... We see in fact a man with glasses, his mouth rather small, with a metal collar that is joined to a space suit of flexible and shiny fabric. We notice mysterious bracelets (...) and a mysterious device on the belly..." Thus starts the text that accompanies two photographs in a book published in Italy in 1963.

The author continues: "Who took these photographs? When? How? Where is this pilot from? What does he eat? What does he drink? Smoke? What is his sexual behavior? What would be the answer to these questions? You will know everything little by little, gradually, in the coming years. (I myself will write details that I cannot reveal now.) What is essential to know for now is that they are men."[1]

The author was Alberto Perego (1903-1981), an Italian diplomat who served as Consul to many countries around the world and who was instrumental in documenting the history of contemporary UFO sightings in Italy and around the world in the 1950s and '60s. Many of the details which he promised here did materialize, but seemingly not in his fourth book, a comprehensive overview of sightings and media reports from 1943-1970, in which he only hinted at the contacts through which he obtained the photographs. The reason? After the publication of his third book in 1963, in which he included these photographs, the Italian Foreign Ministry sent him to Belo Horizonte, as the Italian Consul in Brazil, where he spent his final years in forced isolation, only to come back to Rome a few times in the 1970s to speak at the occasional conference organised by his friend Eufemio del Buono, where Perego finally enjoyed some unexpected public recognition.[2]

On 7 November 2010 he was rehabilitated with the launch of his biography, written by journalist Ivan Ceci, in the prestigious Accademia di Romania, and a comprehensive website about his research into the extraterrestrial presence, called Progetto Perego. Yet, it seems, not everyone is in agreement with his rehabilitation, as the website has been the target of repeated hacking efforts, rendering it offline for lengthy periods of time.

Perego continues his description of the intriguing photographs as follows: "Whether they are beautiful, ugly, tall, short, fat or thin, brown or blond is not really important. They are men, and certainly better than us because of the tolerance and patience demonstrated in the face of our atomic madness.

"We must be grateful to them for the permanent dredging of our atmosphere, which, without them, would have already been irreparably contaminated by residues of our atomic explosions. We must be grateful to them for having prevented, until now, nuclear war.

"Those who have met these extraterrestrial pilots describe them as fascinating for their intelligence, dignity and sympathy, and especially for their sincere and disinterested friendship which they show and which inspires those who have met them. But what would happen if their photographs were published in our newspapers? It would result in a grotesque carnival, worthy of our stupid malignancy."[3]

Alberto Perego was, of course, one of the prominent Italians who was involved in the Amicizia – or Friendship – Case, the

Another photograph of the extraterrestrial pilot. First published in Alberto Perego, *L'aviazione di altri pianeti opera tra noi: rapporto agli italiani: 1943-1963* (Rome, 1963)

true scale and scope of which only became known with the publication of Stefano Breccia's book *Contattismi di Massa* in 2007 (published in English as *Mass Contacts* in 2009).

While the authorities weren't too thrilled about Perego's efforts to disclose whatever information he could find or was privy to in his intended next book, *Dirò tutto* ('Telling all'), it seems he also had a change of heart about telling all, saying: "Either we must transform Ufology into a revolutionary political movement in order to overthrow old establishments, or we acknowledge that we must speak only when necessary, whatever our ideas may be."[4] This reminds us of Adamski's space contacts telling him to use his discretion when sharing his experiences and knowledge with others[5], and it could indicate that Perego was told something similar upon his meeting with extraterrestrials.

That he did have a lot of information is evinced in some of the stunning photographs of flying saucers that appear in his second book, *Sono Extraterrestri!* ("They are extraterrestrial!";

One of the hundreds of photographs taken by the Amiciza contactees.

1958), and Ivan Ceci, his biographer, too, says that Perego knew details about underground bases, interventions with respect to international crises, as well as their physical appearance and some characteristics of their morals and ethics.[6]

More details, however, already emerged through journalist Bruno Ghibaudi in an interview with the Italian weekly *Le Ore* in its latter two editions of January 1963 under the headline: "Bruno Ghibaudi Confirms: Yes, I Have Talked to the Pilots of the Flying Saucers". The interview was translated into English by Gordon W. Creighton and published in *Flying Saucer Review* in June of that year as part of a series titled 'The Italian Scene', which included reports of several other eye-witnesses as well. And while UK researcher and author Timothy Good wrested this translated interview from oblivion by quoting from it in his book *Alien Base* in 1998, he was unaware even then of the historical scope of the case.

Ghibaudi was a well-known journalist in Italy at the time, reporting on aviation and space travel on television and radio. About a year before he took a series of photographs of flying saucers off the coast of Pescara, which for many years was the epicentre of the Italian Amicizia contacts, he was assigned to make a TV programme about people who claimed to have seen UFOs only to find to his utter amazement that, according to Creighton, "in his own country, there were large numbers who had seen them, or taken photos of them, or met the pilots, or secured pieces of metal and other materials left by saucers that landed, and so forth".

In his interview Ghibaudi revealed that he had been invited to meet some of the visitors from space on which occasion several witnesses were present, including the person who had arranged the meeting. From his own experience, he confirmed that the human form is "universal throughout the Cosmos, as part of a general harmony – and yet the idea of this has generally been rejected by Earthmen as impossible, no doubt, *as almost always, the truth is too simple to be accepted.*" Creighton continues his summary of Ghibaudi's interview: "Apart, therefore, from various sorts of superficial differences, Man throughout the Universe resembles us... These space visitors, he says, are coming to our planet at this time of crisis from many different worlds. (…)

"What is happening now is simply that the infant civilization of Earth-Man being at a point of particularly grave crisis, the space beings are prepared to reveal themselves to us more. Ghibaudi confirms, then, their benevolence and their desire to help us. (...) Their aim is to prevent nuclear disaster. Ghibaudi says flatly that they have indicated their firm intention to intervene if it becomes unavoidable."

"Questioned next as to whether such 'human' sentiments as love, hate, friendship, loyalty, solidarity, were found among the extraterrestrials whom he had met, Ghibaudi replied emphatically; 'The experience that I have had of them permits me to affirm that in them the good sentiments are enormously strong, while the bad sentiments are almost entirely absent.'"[7]

Consul Perego was also George Adamski's main contact in Italy. His name and address appear on a 1959 list (reproduced in *George Adamski – A Herald for the Space Brothers*[8]) of national contacts for the international Get Acquainted Program (GAP), which Adamski set up on the advice of his space contacts to foster greater understanding and friendship between people worldwide who were interested in the UFO phenomenon. With the details that have been published about the Friendship Case it is now clear that the Space Brothers themselves were setting up similar efforts, albeit less publicly, in many countries around the world. But as Adamski's mission has been systematically ignored by most researchers, with the notable exception of Timothy Good, so were his GAP efforts, and the obvious link between his programme and Italy's *Caso Amicizia* has thus far gone unnoticed.

According to the excellent documentary *Il Caso Amicizia*, which gives an inspiring dramatic reconstruction of the Friendship Case, a considerable number of space people, who were living and working in underground and underwater bases around Italy, had regular contact with well over a hundred Italians, while similar projects were going on in other European countries and in Siberia, South America and Australia at the same time.[9]

Not long before his death in 2003, the prominent Italian psychologist and theologian Bruno Sammaciccia decided to disclose his experiences with these people from space, that started in 1956 and continued into the late 1970s. While this case, and especially the information coming from the Space Brothers, shows many striking parallels with the information coming from other contactees, it differs in that the humans involved were not invited aboard spacecraft, but rather given access to underground and underwater bases.

Professor Sammaciccia, who held four university degrees and was nominated as UNESCO's 'Man of the Year' in 1982[10], had previously had "extensive experiences in paranormal phenomena" and "had met many Masters from the East". In April 1956, Sammaciccia, who lived in Pescara, Abruzzo, Italy, and two of his friends, Giancarlo, an accountant, and Giulio, an engineer, had a strange experience. They were studying a map of Ascoli Piceno, north-west of Pescara, with regard to a possible treasure hidden in the castle there, when a pen flew out of its penholder and landed on the map. When they took out a piece of paper, the pen wrote: "Now I am going to explain to you who

I am, where I come from, and what I want to ask you; I am here to give you of our goodness and knowledge." All the while they were experiencing a strange "beneficent sensation".[11]

A few days after their strange experience they went to the castle in Ascoli Piceno, where they heard a voice say: "Now, my friends, stay calm, because I am going to have one of us appear. Are you ready or aren't you?" As they met their space friends for the first time, they felt an intense emotion as first one, then a second person appeared from behind a wall. One of the two men, who both spoke Italian, was over 2.5 metres tall, while the other was no more than a metre in height.[12]

Sammaciccia's story forms the main part of the section about the Friendship Case in Stefano Breccia's book *Mass Contacts* and gives many details that capture brilliantly not only the different characters of some of the space people involved, but also the sense of humour displayed by these Space Brothers. One unintentionally amusing episode describes how Dimpietro, a 3-metre tall extraterrestrial, commonly referred to by the friends as "the poplar", decided it was time to introduce himself to Sammaciccia's wife Rafaella. Upon coming home she found Dimpietro sitting on the kitchen floor of their flat in Milan, because he didn't want to scare her with his height. Unfortunately, when she saw the human "poplar" in her kitchen she was so frightened that she fled into the bedroom and remained there until her husband returned. Dimpietro was the commander of the largest base in central eastern Italy, while there were smaller bases below Lake Como near Milan, in Bologna, in Rome, in Pescara, in Pineto, and elsewhere.

On their first encounter the Italian friends were told: "This is a critical time in human history." And: "We are not here to conquer, because there is nothing to conquer. We have been on Earth for many centuries, living in secret bases around the planet." And in response to concerns about their strongly ethical perspective on life compared to that of humans: "Our [goodness] and [truth] will be stronger than human doubts."[13]

"Please let the world know that we have come here with a great love towards you. You speak about love, but you do not know what love is. It is the very basis of life itself."[14]

Fostering friendship

While Professor Breccia was an engineer who thought the technology of the space people most important, Sammaciccia's real interests, writes Breccia, "were in the moral meaning behind the experiences, in the feeling of *amicizia* (friendship) which pervaded everything, in the spiritual nobility shown at all times by our friends..."[15]

The Space Brothers who contacted Sammaciccia and his friends actively worked to foster a sense of friendship and shared responsibility by going through the roundabout process of eliciting the group's help in procuring food, fruits and even materials, which they could have clearly resourced in less conventional ways, if they even needed them at all. Sometimes the friends were reimbursed for the costs of the goods, but it was regularly left up to them to furnish the required funds. In an interview fellow contactee Gaspare de Lama said: "[T]his demands of material could be a game to indirectly ask for Uredda [the energy that is produced by the love between people]. This is my idea, I told it to [Stefano] Breccia and he listened to me and said 'It could really be like this'."[16]

As the Space Brothers taught the group, "Love in its most unselfish sense, as well as ethics, respect and altruism should guide every thought and every action. These values are essential to ensure a safe and healthy evolutionary process – a lesson that humanity has to put in practice, if it is to avoid the risk of terrible self-destruction."[17] According to the space visitors, their main task was to make sure humanity would not use its nuclear arsenal and to help our evolutionary progress, trying to push us to a higher level of understanding, even sharing some of our suffering in the process.

In confirmation of Benjamin Creme's insistence that the space visitors are utterly harmless, author Stefano Breccia, who had some encounters of his own, says in the documentary based on Sammaciccia's account: "They said they were incapable of causing harm to anyone. Even their devices [which were consciously impregnated with their sense of ethics and morality] would refuse to harm anyone. Indeed, they said if they weren't able to avoid hurting someone, then in that case they would self-destruct."[18] What's more, as the Martian Firkon told George Adamski, "...if the issue is merely our lives as against the lives of our brothers – even those belligerent ones of your Earth – we would allow ourselves to be destroyed rather than slay a fellow being."[19]

Over the years the people who had experiences with the Space Brothers grew in number and included people from all walks of life, some of whom rather well-known in Italian society, such as university professors, among whom Paolo di Girolamo, television journalist Bruno Ghibaudi, well-known painter Gaspare de Lama, as well as Alberto Perego, who himself had been one of many eye-witnesses to the appearance of a UFO formation of hundreds of tiny spheres of light in the form of a cross in the sky over the Vatican on 6 November 1954.[20]

In *Flying Saucers Farewell*, his last book about his experiences with UFOs and the space people, George Adamski describes an interesting episode that took place during his visit to Rome on 12 June 1959 where he and his Swiss associate Lou Zinsstag were met at the airport by Alberto Perego. After having had dinner, the party went for a walk before going to their hotel, but by the time they reached a main thoroughfare, there was no taxi to be found as it was already midnight. Following a hunch, Adamski, while unfamiliar with the streets of Rome, suggested they go in a certain direction where "suddenly, out of nowhere, a taxi pulled up". However, writes Adamski, "instead of driving us directly to the hotel, the driver proceeded to take us on a scenic tour of Rome that lasted until nearly daybreak before he finally drew before the hotel. Every moment of the trip had been most enjoyable ... a night I shall never forget!" Remarkably, the driver refused to accept extra fare money, saying "I am glad to do it for the American".[21]

Many similar experiences have been reported in letters to the editor of *Share International* magazine, which, when

From left to right: Alberto Perego, Mario Maioli, who would later become the first General Secretary of the Centro Ufologico Nazionale (CUN), Lou Zinsstag and George Adamski in a restaurant in Rome, June 1959

authentic, are confirmed by Benjamin Creme's Master as an act of support, succour or inspiration by one of the Masters of Wisdom or the World Teacher himself, and indeed, many comparable instances of such 'divine intervention' from history survive in local legends around the world. The driver in the episode described by Adamski was, according to Benjamin Creme's Master, a Space Brother.[22]

While Bruno Sammaciccia refers to the space people as the 'W56', with the number '56' referring to the year when the contacts started, and 'W' being double 'V' for 'Victory', they referred to themselves as 'Akrij' (pronounced 'Aukree'). Interestingly, according to Sammaciccia, the word 'Akrij' in one form or another, has found its way into various terrestrial languages – in Sanskrit it means 'sages', in Egyptian it means 'deities', the Greek form means 'people in high places', while a similar word in Arabic translates as a 'group of friends'.[23]

Author Stefano Breccia states that, despite their obvious scientific advancement, "the W56 weren't acting as superior beings; on the contrary, they were extremely friendly, almost [like] brothers (whence the name that so many people have given them, independently…)."[24] Professor Paolo di Girolamo concurs when he quotes Meredir (or Merhedir, as he spells the name): "Basically we are humans like yourselves, characterized by imperfections and defects, hopes and illusions, so do not make the mistake of considering us 'angels' or 'superior'. But we do value sincerity and friendship greatly."[25]

Elsewhere Breccia adds, about the way they taught the group: "[D]uring our talks, they were exerting a kind of maieutics, extracting from within ourselves concepts that had been kept buried under tons of commonplaces and convenient attitudes. For sure, this has been the most important gift by Amicizia…"[26] Describing how spirituality to them is the basis of everything, Sammaciccia says: "They see God even in the smallest insect ... and that God is everywhere in cosmos. Their religion is not as full of rituality as our cults are; to them it is just a deep feeling [awareness], that doesn't need [outer] appearances."[27]

Worldwide effort

Apart from many details of the space people's advanced technology, knowledge and their control of natural laws reminiscent of the abilities of great avatars and senior disciples (such as Madame Blavatsky), a striking feature of this case is the similarity with George Adamski's Get Acquainted Program (GAP), an international network of contacts who would forward the latest information coming from the Space Brothers through Adamski to interested people in their respective countries. While an in-depth look at Adamski's mission shows that the coming of the UFOs is not an event in itself, but is happening in support of the awakening of humanity to the spiritual realities of life and the return to the everyday world of the Elder Brothers of our Spiritual Hierarchy, as I have shown in my first book, the Friendship Case provides ample evidence that Adamski's GAP was not an isolated attempt, but part of a sustained, worldwide effort by the Space Brothers.

Introducing GAP to his supporters around the world in 1957, Adamski wrote: "Information of the Brothers of other worlds (...) will be sent regularly to each national leader, who in turn will forward it... The idea is that the citizens of each nation, through these efforts, will grow into closer united friendship with their countrymen, without discrimination or divisions of any kind. In time it is hoped that these national efforts will overflow into worldwide understanding and friendship."[28] Likewise, Sammaciccia wrote about the Italian

Friendship Case: "Their idea was to gather a small group of enlightened people (...), and to train them so that they could behave as trainers to their fellows, and so, little by little, our attitudes could change..."[29]

Breccia's book documents that the Friendship efforts were not limited to Italy, but that similar projects were going on in Germany, Switzerland, France, Spain, South America and elsewhere. After hearing about Breccia's plans to publish the story of Bruno Sammaciccia and his friends, one of the main protagonists in Germany contacted Breccia, and the writer added the information from his German contact in his book.

Further information about the Friendship group has emerged through Croatian-born writer and filmmaker Nikola Duper, who was asked by one of the many other participants to go public with the story of Friendship. In a description of the people from space this contactee literally says: "The Friends are our elder brothers. They are human. Indeed, in comparison it's we terrestrials who are less than human. They are much more human than we are..."[30]

This person's testimony also confirms the connection between the various efforts of the space people to help humanity get to grips with the reality of their existence and their visits: "At the end of the '40s, the Friends offered their collaboration to the head of the USA Administration. In exchange, they asked that the nuclear weaponry program be given up. But their offer and request were rejected... Following the American politico-military refusal, the Friends undertook the strategy consisting in confidential contacts with small groups of terrestrials, trying to emphasize the quality of human personal relationships, the value of Love and Uredda, rather than quantity and visibility."[31]

In his story Bruno Sammaciccia relates how the Space Brothers used various devices to facilitate communication between them and the group of terrestrial friends, including a transistor radio to relay their messages. As Stefano Breccia details: "Long distance contacts took place mainly via radio broadcast: these guys were able to send a message to a particular receiver, wiping away the normal broadcast, with incredible selectivity: if one had put two receivers one beside the other, both tuned on the same frequency, only the pre-selected one [would] receive the friends' message, while the other was going on as if nothing was happening!"[32] Many of these were recorded and one of the messages from the Brother referred to as Sigir that is played in the video documentary about the Amicizia case runs as follows:

"Dear friends, dear sons. Do not doubt us, as none of us will waver. Stay united. United. United. Endure your mutual weaknesses, while struggling to improve your humanity and your friendship towards us.

"Our world is hard for you to understand, dear friends. That is natural. However, with affection and trust you can be close to our hearts, which are always open towards you, and understand us more. We embrace you with warm affection and sincere friendship. Yours, Sigir"

Unfortunately, however, over the years, discord arose among the Italian friends and the group eventually broke up, which some of them believe undermined the ability of the 'W56' to withstand their selfish counterparts, the 'contrari' extraterrestrials, or CTR, who were here for less altruistic reasons (see also Chapter 6). The same happened to the 17 GAP chapters around the world, withering with the passing of George Adamski and the character assassination committed on him to the point that most people felt he was best left forgotten.

However, the documentary concludes that the real essence of the experience was "the immense example of love, dedication and respect that [the space people] impressed in the hearts of the eyewitnesses" that are still alive. As Gaspare de Lama, one of the Amicizia participants, says: "They enriched me. They put me into contact with an almost impossible world full of love."

The presence of the Space Brothers and the return of the Masters as our Elder Brothers, however, not only furnish proof, but also *guarantee* that such a "world full of love" is possible. We only need to take their lessons to heart and put them into practice. Or, as Gaspare de Lama puts it elsewhere: "They made me understand that a better world is not utopia, because they [themselves] exist."[33]

The love that he speaks of is not our sentimental notion of love, which so often, even if subconsciously, is possessive and conditional on reciprocation. As Stefano Breccia clarifies, while admitting that he has not had too deep an involvement in the Friendship saga, "[The space people] used to say, 'I am everybody, and everybody is me' ... That small sentence illuminates a concept that we feel within our heart, but refuse to understand: all living entities, from microbes to luminaries, are the very same thing, because they reflect, in one way or another, a single reality, God. What's more, even the so-called inanimate entities are participating in this reality. Therefore the dualism between 'myself' and 'not myself' is meaningless."[34]

Underground bases

Although it may not have been common knowledge in the 1950s and 1960s, the existence of underground bases has been extensively documented in connection with the sighting of UFO activity in the last few decades.

In its edition of 9 January 2005, the *Indian Daily* ran an

article that was titled "China and India both know about underground UFO base in the Himalayan border area deep into the tectonic plates". According to the article, locals from both sides in one of the least accessed areas in the world, the disputed Indo-Chinese border in Ladakh, which by agreement is not patrolled by either country, have reported seeing UFOs coming out of the ground, and both the Indian and the Chinese government are aware of the existence of the extraterrestrial underground base.

The article quotes local guides who say that lighted triangular craft coming from somewhere underground in the area, and moving almost vertically up, is nothing new. When asked by inquisitive pilgrims who had witnessed these lights in the area, Indian border personnel confirmed that strange, lighted objects emerge from underground, and that they were ordered not to allow anyone near. The report added that local people are surprised that the Indian government is trying to hide what is obvious to everyone. When children in a local school entered a drawing contest, the article documents, "more than half of the drawings had to do with strange objects in the sky and some coming out of the mountains."[35]

The Master of Wisdom with whom Benjamin Creme has been working since 1959 has confirmed that the reported sightings were authentic and that the area is a long-standing underground base for spaceships from Mars.[36] Earlier, in April 2000, Benjamin Creme confirmed that similar reports from the province of Cordoba and in the Pampa in Argentina, where villagers talk about "landing platforms" for extraterrestrial visitors with whom they say they interact, were authentic.[37]

In his book *Alien Base – Earth's Encounters with Extraterrestrials*, UK researcher Timothy Good writes about the experiences of a German businessman, Ludwig Pallmann, who said he was taken

Beings of light captured on video in Ongamira, Cordoba, Argentina (Video stills: Mónica Coll and Pablo Dessy; © analuisacid.com)

into an extraterrestrial base on the border of Brazil and Peru. Two years later, in his book *Unearthly Disclosure*, Mr Good wrote a whole chapter about extraterrestrial bases on Earth. Here he writes that George Adamski was told in a private letter from a marine engineer in Alaska "that spacecraft landed on a regular basis in a certain area of that state. The unnamed engineer claimed to have seen humanoid beings there, varying from three to six and a half feet in height." Adds Good: "As I have shown in *Alien Base*, many of Adamski's claims cannot be dismissed."[38]

About an extraterrestrial base at Pine Gap, near Alice Springs, Northern Territory, Australia, Good says he was "reminded of the information given to George Adamski, as long ago as 1949, by a government scientist and former commanding officer in the Chilean Air Force, who claimed that a large 'space laboratory' (…) had been in operation since 1948, and that 'space ships could be landing there [and that] a communication system could be going on through this laboratory between earthmen and spacemen.' (…) As revealed in *Alien Base*, Adamski held a US Government Ordnance Department identification card which gave him access to military bases, and he had regular meetings with military contacts who passed him sensitive information."[39]

In 2010 Pablo Dessy published some remarkable stills from a video taken in the Cordoba province of Argentina, in 2006, where he was among a party of people who were hiking in the Ongamira region, north-east of the capital Buenos Aires. One of them, Mónica Coll, filmed some of her companions from a slightly elevated position at a short distance. Only when she looked at her images at home did she see human figures of light, apparently coming out of the ground through a staircase or exit of light. Neither the beings nor the exit were visible to the people present at the time of filming.[40] When asked, Benjamin Creme confirmed that the images are of Space Brothers, seen in the etheric, who were exiting a solid physical underground structure.[41]

It should be noted that the etheric appearance of people or craft on film or photographs is not haphazard, but subject to a certain purpose which the Space Brothers may have in making themselves visible only after the film or photograph were taken. Similar occurrences are known to have been manifested by the Masters of Wisdom, often as a blessing or to strengthen people's faith.

Benjamin Creme elsewhere explains that the underground bases of the Space Brothers play a part in their efforts to neutralize the destructive effects of the nuclear waste, toxins and other pollutants that we have released into the soil, as much as in the air or in the seas: "They have devices which can neutralize the worst elements of pollution, particularly of high-level nuclear radiation."[42]

Friendship continues

While Bruno Sammaciccia says the contacts of the Italian groups of friends with extraterrestrials continued into the late 1970s, Nikola Duper's informant says they went on until around 1990. Given that the space people had various bases and multiple 'friendship' projects going on around Europe, both may be correct. While several cases of individual contacts took place in Italy regardless, such as Giorgio Dibitonto's in 1980 and Maurizio Cavallo's in 1981, further evidence of the Friendship efforts emerged from South America later in the same decade.

Beginning in 1985 Octavio Ortiz, a Chilean radio ham, was contacted by people who spoke with a foreign accent and who said they were members of a community in one of the most southerly and indomitable territories of southern Chile. Mr Ortiz spent several months talking on radio with these people who presented themselves as the "Servants of the Servants of the Lord" or Servers of "Angels of the Lord", a mysterious community located on the equally mysterious 'Isla Friendship', or 'Friendship Island'.

As the story of Friendship in South America has not received much attention outside the Spanish-speaking world yet, it might be useful to summarize the main facts here, based on the book *Friendship – ¿Evidencias de contacto extraterrestre?*[43] ('Friendship – Evidence of Extraterrestrial Contact?') by Mr Ortiz, the main protagonist, and the extensive research into the case by Spanish UFO researcher Josep Guijarro.[44]

The story of the South American branch of 'Friendship' began in January 1984, when radio amateur Octavio Ortiz of Santiago received an emergency call on his 27MHz radio transmitter from a ship that was deployed by the Department of Oceanography of the University of Chile in Valdivia in the Los Lagos region, the 10th administrative region of Chile. The researchers on the ship had watched in amazement as a huge red ball perched on the water just a few feet away from their ship near the lighthouse of Mitague, in the channel of Moraleda. The crew began to broadcast distress calls to the captaincy in Iquique, which were heard by the Ortiz family, consisting of Octavio and his wife Claudia, and daughters Cristina, Andrea and Paula, who operated their own 27MHz radio station (citizens' band), under the name of 'Lucero' ('Bright Star').

When after about 15 minutes still no response was coming from Iquique, Mr Ortiz offered to serve as a bridge between the ship and the captaincy. The crew told Ortiz to tell the captaincy that the strange object had caused their electrical equipment to malfunction.

Some time after the incident Octavio was contacted by one Alberto, owner of a yacht by the name of Mitilus II, who said he had witnessed the incident. Alberto later also told Octavio that he had been in contact with a mysterious community of highly ethical or spiritual scientists who showed great mental abilities and who called their community 'Friendship'. Through Alberto, Octavio eventually got in touch with members of Friendship with whom well over 1,200 hours of radio communication have been recorded over the years.

On 17 August 1985, at 2:30pm, Octavio's wife Claudia was told, in one of these communications, to "go outside and look at the sky". When Claudia went outside she saw a bright object. Amazingly, the "caller", by the name of 'Ariel' began to tell her how he would have the UFO move, to how many degrees and in which direction, until Cristina warned not to go near an airplane flying nearby. In addition to being seen by other witnesses, the sighting was also filmed by TV cameras of Televisión Nacional de Chile (TVN) and seen by officials of the meteorological department who could offer no explanation.

Separately, former director of technical services for Chilean radio and television Ernesto de la Fuente, who had moved to the island of Chiloé in the 1980s, also came into contact with Alberto. The area around Chiloé is known for its frequent UFO sightings and the residents, mainly fishermen, are used to seeing UFOs there. According to the 1999 documentary *La Isla de Friendship* made by Chile's TVN channel[45], the Mitilus II could not be found in the official ship registers of Chile, but Mr De la Fuente says it measured 42 feet in length, was recently refurbished and painted white. There is also a sergeant of the Chilean marine in the Castro region, where Chiloé is located, who confirms that he saw a ship by the name of Mitilus II near the port of Melinka one night in 1992. For what he saw, most of the crew did not look like Chileans but instead were tall with a fair complexion and blue eyes. As the ship did not dock at Melinka, no record was entered in the port's register.

Months after his first contacts with Octavio Ortiz and Ariel, Ernesto de la Fuente, who had been a chain smoker until that time, was diagnosed with lung cancer by doctors at the Catholic University of Santiago de Chile. Ariel assured Ernesto that the Space Brothers could cure him and allowed him to travel to the island aboard the Mitilus II. He embarked in a bay a few kilometers south of Quemchi, where Alberto had taken passengers to the island before. They sailed southward, passing Quillón and Melinka and after about a day and a half they arrived in a narrow channel that was no more than 20 meters wide, with cliffs and vegetation on both sides.

At the end of the channel was a pier where they disembarked and passed a rustic wooden portico before entering a room that was excavated in the rock. They then passed into another room and took an elevator down. According to Ernesto there were 14 extraterrestrials and 60 other visitors like him, not all Chilean but from different Latin American countries, also for treatment. According to Mr De la Fuente the extraterrestrials were all nearly 2 meters tall, of fair complexion and blond, and their eyes radiated peace and serenity. They told him they were there because they were the servers of the "Servers of the Lord".

After four days of treatment he was healed and after another two days of convalescence he left again. Within ten days of leaving his home as a terminal patient Ernesto de la Fuente returned a healed man.[46]

In his book *Isla Friendship – Conexion OVNI*, Mr De la Fuente writes: "Everything that the Friendship Community do is based on their spiritual beliefs, that is their reason for being. Their technical-scientific work is done with that motivation. The

Friendship religion is by no means secret, rather it is one of the best-known philosophies of the world, and one of the least observed: it is the one that the Christ brought. The great difference is that they are hundreds of years ahead of us in technology, and thousands of years ahead of us in spirituality. They practice what they preach. They teach that the body is our temple, however I know that after a certain time, only few can visit a very sacred place, or Temple, which they say is very far away, and is the House where God lives. Here I have to stress that they are talking about the 'Angels of God', the extraterrestrial beings that are in contact with the residents of Friendship Island."[47]

Skeptics, whose attitude generally doesn't make them the best candidates for finding evidence or even making useful connections, point out that there is no island that would fit the descriptions and, on the island that has been identified by some as Friendship Island there is nothing to be found that would indicate habitation. As will be shown in Chapter 5, however, the extraterrestrial visitors do not depend for most of their work on a solid physical body (or craft). What is more, those who have mastered their lower nature, also have control over the laws of nature and physics to the point that they can apparently 'bend' the space of their location so as to become invisible or untraceable.

An astounding example of this can be found in Sylvia Cranston's monumental biography of H.P. Blavatsky, in the chapter which describes HPB's arrival in Bombay (Mumbai), India. In March 1879, about a month after she had arrived from the United States, HPB got into a buggy with her assistant Moolji. Instead of telling him where they were going, she would tell him to order the driver to go left, right or straight ahead at every turn of the route, until they had reached a suburb of Bombay where roads and paths crossed in the wood, while

HPB continued to give directions unfalteringly to "a private estate, with a magnificent rose garden in front and a fine bungalow with spacious Eastern verandahs in the background."

Mystified that he, as a Bombay resident, had not known about the existence of such a magnificent poperty so close to the city, the assistant told his friends of his amazement. They laid a wager that there was no such bungalow in that area and that Moolji could not lead them there. When Moolji insisted he could retrace every turn of the way they set out, only for Moolji to feel "completely baffled" when the bungalow was nowhere to be found. HPB later told her associates that "the bungalow, like all other spots inhabited by Adepts, was always protected from the intrusion of strangers by a circle of illusion formed about it..."[48]

The chronicle from which HPB's biographer quoted this episode adds: "All the buried ancient libraries, and those vast hoards of treasure which must be kept hidden until its Karma requires its restoration to human use, are protected from discovery by the profane, by illusory pictures of solid rocks, unbroken solid ground, a yawning chasm, or some such obstacle, which turns aside the feet of the wrong men, but which Mâyâ [the Hindu goddess of illusion] dissolves away when the predestined finder comes to the spot in the fullness of time."

More friendship from space

As mortal humans we are no strangers to the concept of changing the appearance of things we hold dear and wish to protect from the attacks of our less sensitive – or sensible – fellows. Some things we know to harbour the truth because they lift up our hearts and our spirits beyond our 'natural' state, even if we can't prove that they do so. When that happens, we don't need external confirmation – we know, because the truth rings so loud in our soul. After all, Reality can't be proven; it can only be experienced. Einstein often "intuited" aspects of Reality which he then had to work years on to prove in mathematical formulas or equations. So we could say that proof of something is necessary mostly for people who do not yet have the experience of that aspect of Reality.

Something similar pertains when one reads Enrique Barrios' book *Ami, Child of the Stars* that, disguised as a children's story, explains the secrets of life and the universe. Better, reading it helps one experience the secrets of life and the universe, leaving the reader with the same sense of joy and oneness as, for instance, listening to Beethoven's *An die Freude* ('Ode to Joy') – which, not co-incidentally, is a celebration of the brotherhood of man.

Barrios wrote this book in response to an experience which he had in August 1985, which he has never given details or answered questions about. He was suggested, it seems, to write about it "as if it were a children's story, a fantasy … otherwise they will think you are a liar or crazy."[49] Indeed, apparently well aware of the problems that the current volume intends to counter, in the opening words of his book the author says his friend from space "warned me that few adults will understand this book, because for them it's easier to believe in horror than in wonder. To avoid problems, he advised me to say that this is only a fairy tale. I'll do as he said: THIS IS A STORY FOR CHILDREN, WHICH MEANS ALL OF US."[50] Thereby in effect saying that the narrative device is just that – a narrative device.

So Mr Barrios tells the story of the protagonist 'Pete' ('Pedro' in the original Spanish and 'Jim' in the second English edition), a 10-year-old boy, who sees a UFO disappear in the sea and what he thinks is a child come onto the beach. When asked for his name, the extraterrestrial tells Pete: "You can call me 'Amigo' for friend; because that's what I am: a friend to all."

Pete decides to call his new friend Ami, short for the Spanish words 'Amigo' (friend) or 'Amistad' (friendship). Echoing the testimonies of president Ilyumzhinov of Kalmykia, Pope John XXIII's assistant, and the contactees of the 1950s (see Chapter 3), Ami tells Pete: "The human model is universal – head, trunk and extremities – but there are small variations on each world: height, skin, color, shape of the ears, small differences." As they get to know each other, Pete surmises that his new friend is not a child, but rather an extraterrestrial of a small race. (Indeed, Breccia states that "the most conspicuous difference was in their heights, from six meters to 10 cm."[51])

In an exchange that brims with the innocence of child-like simplicity, and as a result manages to stir one's innermost being through wisdom and humour, Ami helps Pete to expand his understanding of life, while at the same time helping to increase the reader's awareness. For example, when they go for a midnight stroll through Pete's village, Ami tells Pete: "Look how the light falls on that vine... see those antennas outlined against the stars... Life has no purpose other than enjoyment, Pete. Make sure to pay attention to all that life offers... The wonder that each instant brings... The most profound meaning of life is found beyond thought..." In response, his terrestrial friend writes: "His words made me see things in a new way. It seemed incredible to me that this world was my own place, the everyday one, to which I hardly paid attention."[52]

Speaking about God, Ami explains, "God doesn't have a human appearance. He has no form at all. He is not a person like you or me. He is an Infinite Being, pure creative energy... pure love... Because of that, the universe is beautiful and good, it is marvellous." Therefore, even the 'evil' people on this planet will become good someday, according to Ami.[53]

As Pete wondered why the people from space don't act to

avert catastrophe on Earth because of the pollution, the risk of nuclear war and the depletion of our natural resources, such as "landing a thousand ships and tell the world leaders not to make war", Ami tells Pete that if there would be a mass landing, "thousands of people would die of shock. Remember all your movies about invaders? We are not inhumane, we wouldn't want to cause something like that." When asked why the extraterrestrials don't take over the Earth to make us live in peace, Ami adds: "Human freedom is sacred. 'To force' does not exist in our vocabulary."[54] There is, however, a 'plan of assistance' that the space people "administer in doses, soft, subtly... very subtly" by allowing us to sight their ships shortly after the first atomic tests and explosions. "Later, we increased the frequency of the sightings. Soon we will let your people begin to film us."[55]

One of the reasons why UFOs will allow themselves to be sighted, but refrain from entering into communication, according to Ami, is that many people on Earth are prone to idolatry: "We would be lacking in respect if we claimed to usurp God's place before the misguided religion of those poor people... If they considered us brothers, that would be another story..."[56] A similar notion was conveyed by Stefano Breccia, who wrote: "[N]otwithstanding the scientific gap between them and their friends from Earth, the W56 weren't acting as superior beings; on the contrary, they were extremely friendly, almost like brothers..."[57]

The 'plan of assistance' also involves lending "a hand in the birth of religions that lead to love..."[58] According to Ami, the state of development of a planet depends on the number of its people who have more than a certain "amount of love". At a certain point he shows Pete what that looks like in a man they are observing from Ami's ship, through his advanced instruments: "The man appeared on another screen, but he looked almost transparent. In the middle of his chest shone a golden light..."[59], which reminds us of the 'Uredda' that the extraterrestrials taught their Italian contacts about.

The involvement of the space people with the developments on Earth seems to be an expression of exactly this measure of love in the cosmic brothers and sisters. As Ami explains: "The evolved worlds form a universal brotherhood; we are all brothers, from whatever corner of the cosmos, and all are free to come and go without hurting anyone. (...) There are no galactic wars, no violence among ourselves (...) There is no competition among us, no one wishes to be more than your brother, the only thing we all want is to enjoy life; but since we love, we derive our greatest joy from serving, helping others, being useful to them, and being useful we are joyful."

Ami continues: "Life is very simple for us, though we may have many scientific advances. If the people of Earth manage to survive, if they are able to overcome their mistrust, we will present ourselves from many corners of the universe to help them, to integrate into the cosmic brotherhood."[60]

At a certain point Ami asks Pete what part of his body he points to when he says 'I'. As Pete is lost for an answer to Ami's follow-up question why people point to their chest, Ami tells him: "Because that's where you are, really, you. You are love and love is born in the chest... Only God is perfect, pure love, but we are a spark of divine love and we should try to approach that which we really are..."[61] According to the age-old Wisdom teachings the heart chakra, which is the 'spiritual heart', or the heart of the wise man at the right side of the chest in the Bible[62], is where the human soul connects with its vehicle in the three worlds, the personality.

The UFO seen over Jerusalem on 28 January 2011 was one of the four modern-day 'stars of Bethlehem' that were announced by Benjamin Creme in December 2008, which herald the open emergence of the World Teacher, Maitreya. The red-orange balls of light that were seen were smaller spacecraft servicing the 'star'. (Source: *Share International* magazine, March 2011, p.13)

False divisions

It should be remembered, again, that we are not talking of 'love' as some vague and sentimental idea here, but rather as the glue of the universe, the force in nature that holds galaxies and communities together, and which needs to be expressed in society through harmlessness in our relations with others, by putting into practice the realization that we are One human race and ensuring that the basic needs of every man, woman and child – for adequate food, shelter, healthcare and education – are met. The love that all teachers of humanity – terrestrial or extraterrestrial – speak of, must be expressed on a practical level as freedom and justice for everyone.

A stunning display of the Space Brothers' endorsement of this universal truth, the Golden Rule, happened when a bright white UFO was filmed by at least three different people as it appeared over the Temple Mount in Jerusalem in the early hours of 28 January 2011, during the massive popular uprising in Egypt and elsewhere in the Middle East as an expression of the people's desire for freedom and justice.

Although some doubted the authenticity because they felt the space people would never incite disharmony by appearing over such a contested location, its occurrence could in fact not have been more pertinent and timely. The very fact that it appeared over the Temple Mount, which is claimed as a holy place by three of the major religions of the world, seems symbolic of what George Adamski said about the Space Brothers, that "...they recognize no false divisions of any kind..."[63]

From a spiritual point of view this is another example of the Space Brothers' higher sense of balance and impartiality toward our petty conflicts, in a show of support for the legitimate demands of the people for the universal ideals of justice and freedom, as recorded in the reports of all the early contactees.

It is noteworthy in this context that, according to Benjamin Creme's Master, this sighting involved one of the four specially commissioned spacecraft that have been positioned in the four corners of the globe as modern-day 'stars of Bethlehem', to herald the final phase of the World Teacher's emergence into full public view through a series of television interviews which started in 2009 in the US.[64] Another sighting of a UFO over the Temple Mount two months later, on 28 March 2011, involved a 'regular' space craft.[65]

Notes:

1 Alberto Perego (1963), *L' aviazione di altri pianeti opera tra noi : rapporto agli italiani: 1943-1963*, pp.532-534

2 Biographical note on Alberto Perego, on the Progetto Perego website <www.progettoperego.itindex.php?option=com_content&view=article&id=4 &Itemid=4> [Accessed 17 August 2011]

3 Perego (1963), op cit.

4 Roberto Pinotti, Foreword to Stefano Breccia (2009), *Mass Contacts*, p.8

5 George Adamski (1955), *Inside the Space Ships*, p.102

6 Ivan Ceci (2011), 'Perego, il console degli UFO'. *Corriere della Sera*, [online] 16 February. Available at <misterobufo.corriere.it/2011/02/ 16/ufo_xfiles_avvistamenti_ovni_incontri_ravvicinati_et_ abduction_amicizia_dischi_ volanti_alieni_extraterrestri/> (updated) [Accessed 19 August 2011]

7 Gordon W. Creighton (1963), 'The Italian Scene – Part 3: Bruno Ghibaudi's contact claim'. *Flying Saucer Review* Vol.9, No.3, May-June, p.19

8 Gerard Aartsen (2010), *George Adamski – A Herald for the Space Brothers*, p.62

9 Luca Trovellesi Cesana (dir.; 2010), *Il Caso Amicizia*

10 Paola Harris (2009), 'Italy's disclosure of human looking aliens!' [online] Available at <www.paolaharris.com/timing.htm> [Accessed 10 March 2011]

11 Stefano Breccia (2009), *Mass Contacts*, pp.166-67

12 Ibidem, pp.170-71

13 Ibid., p.172

14 Ibid., p.186

Fostering friendship

15 Breccia (2009), op cit, p.160
16 Ceci (2011a), 'Witness of Italian extraterrestrial contact case emerges'. ExoNews, [online] 15 August. Available at <news.exopoliticsinstitute.org/index.php/interview-with-italian-witness-of-et-contact91/> [Accessed 3 September 2011]
17 Trovellesi Cesana (dir.; 2010), op cit
18 Ibid.
19 Adamski (1955), op cit, p.79
20 Perego (1963), op cit, pp.89-92
21 Adamski (1961), *Flying Saucers Farewell*, pp.171-72
22 Benjamin Creme (2011), answer to question (unpublished)
23 Breccia (2009), op cit, p.227
24 Ibid., p.249
25 Paolo di Girolamo (2009), *Noi e Loro*, p.71
26 Breccia (2009), op cit, p.298
27 Ibid, p.237

Worldwide effort

28 Adamski, letter to associates dated 15 July 1957, as reprinted in Daniel Ross (ed.), *UFOs and Space Science*, No.1, December 1989, p.20
29 Breccia (2009), op cit, p.246
30 Nikola Duper (n.d.), 'The story of "Friendship"', [online], p.2. Available at <w56.duper.org/doc/Friendship.pdf> [Accessed 19 August 2011]
31 Ibid., p.7
32 Breccia (2009), op cit, p.250
33 Ceci (2011a), op cit
34 Breccia (2009), op cit, p.294

Underground bases

35 *India Daily* (2005), 'China and India both know about underground UFO base in the Himalayan border area deep into the tectonic plates'. [online] 9 January. Available at <www.indiadaily.com/editorial/01-09a-05.asp> [Accessed 3 September 2011]
36 Creme (ed.; 2005), 'Signs of the time'. *Share International* Vol.24, No.3, April, pp.18, 23
37 Creme (2001), *The Great Approach – New Light and Life for Humanity*, pp.134-35
38 Timothy Good (2000), *Unearthly Disclosure*, p.256
39 Ibid., p.262
40 Pablo Dessy (2009), '¿Seres de luz en Ongamira?'. Ana Luisa Cid blog [online] 8 August. Available at <analuisacid.com/?p=629> [Accessed 12 March 2011]

41 Aartsen (2011), 'The Friendship Case: Space Brothers teach lessons of brotherhood'. *Share International* magazine Vol.30, No.3, April, pp.11-13

42 Creme (2010), *The Gathering of the Forces of Light – UFOs and their Spiritual Mission*, p.30

Friendship continues

43 Octavio Ortiz (2010), *Friendship – ¿Evidencias de contacto extraterrestre?*

44 Published in the Spanish magazine *Karma-7*, No.292, June 1998

45 See <www.youtube.com/watch?v=tNKbamQwvRY>

46 Televisión Nacional de Chile (TVN, 1999), *La Isla de Friendship*

47 Ernesto de la Fuente (2001), *Isla Friendship – Conexion OVNI*, pp.123-24. Published as PDF: <www.youblisher.com/p/91249-Isla-Friendship/>

48 Henry S. Olcott (1895), *Old Diary Leaves: The True Story of the Theosophical Society*, Second Series, 1878-83, p.45, as quoted in Sylvia Cranston (1993), *HPB – The Extraordinary Life and Influence of Helena Blavatsky, Founder of the Modern Theosophical Movement*, pp.200-01

More friendship from space

49 Enrique Barrios (1989), *Ami, Child of the Stars*, p.34

50 Ibid., p.6

51 Breccia (2009), op cit, p.249

52 Barrios (1989), op cit, p.30

53 Ibid., p.28

54 Ibid., p.26

55 Ibid., pp.32-33

56 Ibid., pp.54-55

57 Breccia (2009), op cit, p.249

58 Barrios (1989), op cit, p.75

59 Ibid., p.50

60 Ibid., p.86

61 Ibid., p.105

62 Ecclesiastes 10:2

False divisions

63 Adamski (1957-58), *Cosmic Science for the Promotion of Cosmic Principles and Truths*, Part 1, Question #6

64 Creme (ed.; 2011), op cit, Vol.30, No.2, March, p.13

65 Ibid., No.4, May, p.11

5. Inside the space ships

Among the many amazing details in the Italian Friendship Case is the description by some contactees of how the space people build their underground bases: by amassing the molecules of the Earth's matter where they want to create a certain space, and compressing these into solid walls.

There was one huge base which was said to be located very deep, on the bottom of the continental plate, which was a hub for all the European activities of the extraterrestrials and which hosted mainly machinery. The smaller bases were used as living places. According to the German Friendship protagonist 'Hans', as quoted in Stefano Breccia's book *Mass Contacts*, the space people use magnetic forces to generate a structure in which the lines of force of the matter used were tightly intertwined. This procedure "had the property of 'opening' matter" so that, by compressing it sideways, or "squashing it [in] on itself", translucent walls resulted "with an astronomical density … and an unbelievable strength. This way they were able to open the cavities that were to become their bases, evidently without damaging in any way the tectonic structures around [it]. (…) Such a structure remained stable [as long as] the fields that had generated it were active". It took a mere flick of a switch to return the area to its original state.[1]

Entering the underground bases seemed to be quite an experience, as Bruno Sammaciccia describes: "I started feeling that the ground under my feet was sort of trembling, the same sensation you feel when you are near a pneumatic drill in action; I was afraid there may be an empty room below us, and that the ground was going to collapse under our weight. But the ground opened itself, and somebody came out. [The man] told us to proceed toward the empty area in the center of the hole through which he had ascended; I was afraid I would fall down into it, but he told us to place our feet in certain areas (there was nothing at all visible there); I did so, and felt as if some invisible step was preventing me from falling into the pit. Then this invisible floor started lowering into the vertical corridor."[2]

A striking parallel can be found in a description by Maurizio Cavallo, author of *Beyond Heaven – A Story of Contact*, of his experience of being taken into an underwater basis in 2005, in an interview with Paola Harris: "[W]e went to a certain point in the sea and then the water around started to whirl; I was scared, of course, because it looked like a hurricane, then we and our boat started to go down. While I was going down, all around me I could see a crystal wall, water was liquid no more, it was solid. Water walls were solid like a tunnel and we went down till a point where those walls opened like rays."[3]

While Sammaciccia, German Friendship contactee 'Hans' and Cavallo describe the bases and their entrances in material terms – and some bases seem to be solid physical structures underneath the Earth's surface[4] – many are in fact etheric physical structures, which do not require the displacement of physical matter, but merely the 'bending' of the solid physical matter as in the description in the opening of this chapter.

The existence of planes of matter above the three that our current science recognizes is not new to students of the Ageless Wisdom teaching. According to these teachings, there are four levels of physical matter above the solid, liquid and gaseous –

known as the etheric physical planes of matter, where atoms vibrate at a higher frequency than on the level immediately below it, just as the molecules of ice, water and vapour vibrate at different frequencies.

Dense physical forms are the precipitation of the blueprints that exist on the etheric physical levels, which is not so esoteric a notion anymore since British biologist Rupert Sheldrake posited the idea of "morphogenetic fields" – a sort of memory bank from where nature retrieves its various solid physical forms.[5] This should also make it easier to understand that Life is not solely dependent on dense physical forms for its expression – it could just as well express itself in etheric physical forms, as indeed it does on the other planets in our solar system, according to the teachings.

In fact, as Giorgio Dibitonto was told by Firkon, the person from Mars whom George Adamski had also met, "The universe contains boundless regions beyond the material one that you know. The only dimension that is observed by your science is the material. … In the cosmos there is not only the material dimension. There are ultra-material dimensions that encompass not only length, breadth and depth, but a much greater richness of life-realities, as a consequence of which all of that which you call behind, in front of, over, under, within and without, become outmoded concepts. The higher a universe is, the more its life-force expresses itself in new, free forms, and the consciousness extends itself to a more comprehensive point of view."[6]

The problem lies, of course, in the fact that the etheric physical eludes the range of vision of most people – although the same is true for electricity or magnetism, which we have got used to and have no problems in accepting as a reality. However, it seems that, gradually, more and more people are able to see auras, while Semyon Kirlian's technology to record the energy fields surrounding living entities was later further developed to photograph human auras. In his article 'The Discovery of the Orgone', the Austrian doctor Wilhelm Reich quotes the German biologist Kammerer, who said that "the existence of a specific life force seems highly probable to me! That is, an energy which is neither heat, electricity, magnetism, kinetic energy (...) nor a combination of any or all of them, but an energy which specifically belongs only to those processes that we call 'life'. That does not mean that this energy is restricted to those natural bodies which we call 'living beings'..."[7] Through experiments Reich subsequently established that the orgone radiation, as he called this primordial life force, permeates everything.

Although Reich was imprisoned by the FBI in the 1950s and left to die there, according to Benjamin Creme the all-penetrating 'orgone radiation' which Reich discovered are in fact the etheric planes of matter which modern-day scientists are on the verge of discovering in their 27 km long particle accelerator – the Large Hadron Collider on the French-Swiss border – and that the 96 per cent of the universe is made up of which was first speculated by Swiss astronomer Fritz Zwicky in the 1930s to be 'dark matter', while his hypothesis later had to be expanded with the notion of 'dark energy'.

The concept of the etheric planes of matter is crucial in this respect. Benjamin Creme even says that, "[u]nless one understands the reality of the etheric levels of energy as finer, subtler, levels of matter, one cannot begin to understand the UFO phenomenon, or the creation of crop circles – because they are all related."[8] However, the principle of space craft becoming visible by lowering the rate of vibration of their atoms, or disappearing from our sight when they return the rate of vibration to its original state, is really not very difficult to understand when Enrique Barrios' protagonist

Ami explains it to his Earth friend Pete: "If a bicycle wheel turns rapidly, you can't see the spokes. We make the molecules of the ship move rapidly."[9]

As I argued in my book *George Adamski – A Herald for the Space Brothers*, even though he was aware of the difference between the levels of solid physical and etheric physical matter, Adamski declined to make that distinction because his experiences and his message were in danger of being obfuscated by a deluge of claims from mystics who said they were receiving "messages" from the space people, while it was Adamski's mission to show the world that they are real, physical (albeit etheric physical) beings.[10] At the same time, he said, in answer to a question whether the space people are 'etherians' or spirits living on different planes: "Space itself is invisible, yet moving within it are natural bodies in varying degrees of density, activated by the ether waves of space. But according to those who have traveled these ether waves, there are no people, 'etherians' or otherwise, living in space itself"[11], i.e. outside the celestial bodies themselves.

To emphasize the physical reality of the space people whom he met, George Adamski told his one-time co-author Desmond Leslie: "They are not goddam spooks".[12] On other occasions, according to author Timothy Good, he would bolster his argument by asking: "Why would a spook need a spaceship?"[13] Indeed, it must be said that many of the space people who come to Earth to help us are highly evolved beings, some of them Masters of Wisdom within the Spiritual Hierarchy of their home planets, as corroborated by Adamski's description in his 1955 book *Inside the Space Ships*, who can travel anywhere by thought. However, according to Benjamin Creme, in order to help us in all the various ways that they do, they need the technology of their space ships. In fact, Creme says, "Many of

A space ship from Jupiter, photographed on 16 February 1989 in the Valle Sagrado Urubamba, Cuzco, Peru. The ship was not visible to the anonymous photographer or the people in the photograph. According to Benjamin Creme's Master the image of the ship, which was in etheric matter, was projected onto the film by the ship's crew, which totalled about 500.

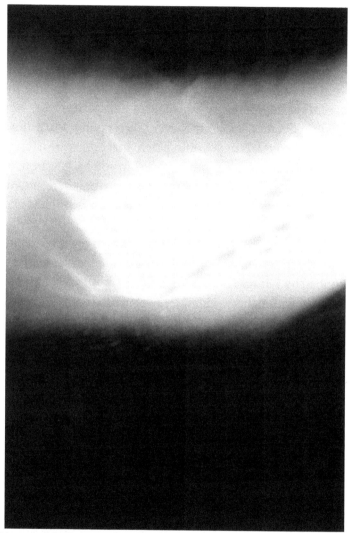

This second photograph was taken a little higher up the mountain. (Photographs first published in *Share International* magazine, November 1994, p.17)

George Adamski gave a very close description of this kind of craft in 1949: "She has a chisel type nose and a fan shape tail. She has fins on her, something like fish, very close to the body." (*Pioneers of Space*, p.123) the large ships (they can be up to four miles long) are mother ships, laboratories and so on."[14]

The fact that they are in etheric physical matter precludes the possibility of anyone being abducted for gene harvesting, hybrid breeding, implanting devices, and other atrocities that the scare-mongering crowd accuses the visitors of. Says Benjamin Creme: "Nobody is ever taken up in a spaceship in a physical body. It is impossible. These spaceships are not solid physical. To be taken up into a spaceship you have to be taken out of the dense physical body and you go in the etheric into the spaceship, which are in themselves etheric. It is still physical, but etheric physical."[15]

The heightened state of awareness which one experiences in the etheric, free from the bonds of dense-physical matter, is described by Giorgio Dibitonto in his book *Angels in Starships*: "The light within this wonderful ray-ship produced an effect on us which I was unable to explain. We felt freshened and renewed, and all our spiritual energies rejoiced in an indescribable sense of peace. At the same time, we found ourselves in a state of well-being which changed us and awakened all the sleeping powers within us. We felt keenly receptive to all that might be imparted to us by words and images. Our hearts burnt with an all-inclusive love, such as is rarely felt on Earth."[16]

However, the experience of being taken out of the body is not often included in how contactees describe their journeys on space craft, and when it is, it is more often than not misunderstood. It takes an esotericist to explain what happened, such as in the well-known case of Travis Walton who had an encounter in 1975. Benjamin Creme, for instance, states that Walton, who was not abducted but invited, and boarded the craft of his own free will, was taken out of his physical body, "which was rendered invisible and protected", while he was taken, in his etheric physical body, on board a mother ship where he had his experiences.[17] According to Benjamin Creme he was asked to tell the world his story, but refrained because he was afraid of ridicule.

The negative memories that some contactees seem to have may be explained by what Adamski said in this respect: "When (...) a person is invited to approach or enter [a space ship] the powerful radiation (force field) is cut down to a minimum. But (...) fear is a destructive force which can kill. And it is my opinion that any reported injuries from space craft are the result of fear rather than radiation from the ships."[18]

Orfeo Angelucci also seems to give some impression of what it must feel like once one is in this 'unearthly' state: "The interior was made of an ethereal mother-of-pearl stuff, irridescent [sic] with exquisite colors that gave off light... There was a reclining chair directly across from the entrance. It was made of the same translucent, shimmering substance – a stuff so evanescent that it didn't appear to be material reality as we know it... As I sat down I marveled at the texture of the material. Seated therein, I felt suspended in air, for the substance of that chair molded itself to fit every surface or movement of my body. As I leaned back and relaxed, that feeling of peace and well-being intensified."[19]

The similarities of the descriptions in Angelucci's 1955 book *The Secret of the Saucers* with those of other contactees are striking. For instance, Dibitonto writes: "The central room was illuminated with light that seemed to come from all directions, as no single light source was to be seen. ... An unaccustomed empathy prevailed; we were all flooded with this same unearthly light, and with an energy that was more spiritual than physical."[20]

George Adamski described the interior of a disk as follows: "Within the craft there was not a single dark corner. I could not make out where the light was coming from. It seemed to permeate every cavity and corner with a soft pleasing glow. There is no way of describing that light exactly. It was not white, nor was it blue, nor was it exactly any other color that I could name."[21] The interior of a mother ship was described by Adamski as a "familiar bluish-white diffused light and the same kind of glassy translucent metal walls."[22]

In his *Cosmic Science* bulletin Adamski later described being taken on board a saucer that incorporated the latest technology: "These visitors, despite the fact that they have traveled space for centuries, are constantly improving their craft. In May of 1957 I had the privilege of examining and riding in one of their latest ships during its maiden voyage. The diameter of this ship was about half again that of the first Venusian scout I described in *Inside the Space Ships*. There was no magnetic pole running through the center, nor did it have a floor lens. These had been replaced with more advanced instruments. They have also perfected a new innovation which is capable of picturing the reactions of people on the ground toward whom they are directing their thoughts."[23]

The latter are quite commonly known among UFO researchers, and preliminary models were explained to Adamski by the pilot on a Saturnian mothership, as described in *Inside the Space Ships*: "The disks are now hovering above a certain inhabited spot on Earth and registering the sounds emanating from that spot. This is what you are seeing on the screen as shown by the lines, dots and dashes. The other machines are assembling this information and interpreting it by producing pictures of the meanings of the signals, together with the original sounds." The workings of the discs were further explained by Zuhl, as follows: "Everything in the Universe has its own particular pattern. For example, if someone speaks the word 'house,' the mental image of a dwelling of one kind or another is in his mind. Many things, including human emotions, are registered in the same way.

"By the use of these machines, we know even what your people are thinking, and whether or not they are hostile toward us. For if there are harsh, frightening words, or even thoughts, these will picture themselves in that manner and our recorders will pick them up accurately. In the same way, we know who amongst you will prove friendly and receptive. Everything in the entire Universe moves by 'vibration,' as you have called it on Earth – or, more recently, 'frequencies.'"[24] Here we are reminded of the work of researchers Masuru Emoto and Andreas Lauterwasser, which is briefly referenced in Chapter 6.

In his 1958 book *Sono Extraterrestri!* ('They are extra-terrestrial!') Italian consul and UFO researcher Alberto Perego included photographs of the interior of the control cabin of a flying saucer that was rendered visible while landing in Francavilla (on the Adriatic Coast) in October 1957. He reports that the diameter of the disc was about 24 meters; that of the cabin 10 meters. About the origin of the photographs (reproduced here on pages 100-103*), Perego writes: "Two men, whom I have known for a long time, entered the disk twice. They were allowed by the pilots to take photographs, but the pilots were not present in the cabin, only their voices could be heard through a loudspeaker. The seats were very high from the ground. From this fact the photographers deduced that the pilots were very tall."[25] This latter fact was later confirmed in Bruno Sammaciccia's account of the Friendship Case.

*The photographs on the following pages were taken by anonymous participants in the Friendship Case and have been digitally enhanced for enlarged reproduction in the current volume. They may not be reproduced from this volume without prior written permission from the author.

The photographs on pages 100-103 show the interior of a flying saucer, for which Alberto Perego gave the following details:

"A kind of table in the centre surmounted by a sphere that pulsates light (at intervals). It seems that the sphere showed the position of the disk in relation to the planet, and that an enlarged view of the fly-over areas is shown on the 'table'."

(Alberto Perego, *Sono Extraterrestri!*, Italy 1958)

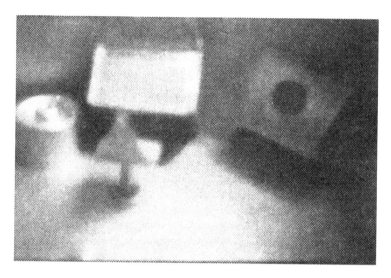

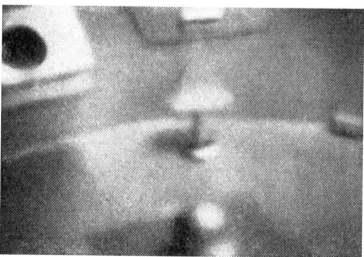

"A seat with a triangular back rest, placed in front of a 'control panel'. To the right there is a kind of monitor next to another device (use unknown)." (Alberto Perego, *Sono Extraterrestri!*, Italy 1958)

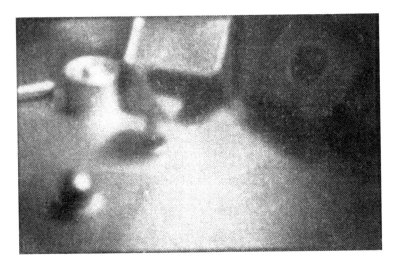

"To the left of the 'control panel' a kind of metal dust bin (use unknown), and a cylinder placed on the ground (use unknown), and further to the left another seat similar to the first one, in front of a small rectangular luminous quadrant. Then another device similar to a monitor."
(Alberto Perego, *Sono Extraterrestri!*, Italy 1958)

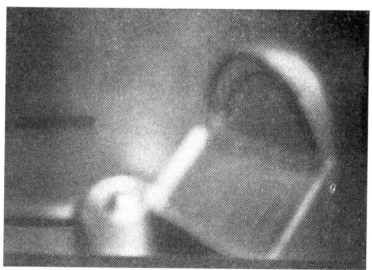

The last two photographs show the 'control panel', luminous [top] and switched off [bottom].
(Alberto Perego, *Sono Extraterrestri!*, Italy 1958)

Space travel

According to George Adamski, "The early crashes [of UFOs] were caused when [nuclear] radiation in our atmosphere was taken into their craft through a process similar to our air conditioning systems. The crews became ill and lost control of their ships, resulting in fatal crashes. After a number of these fatalities had taken place, the crews on other ships began studying conditions and seeking ways to avoid such disasters. Now they have succeeded."

"They have perfected a small object which each crew member carries on his person while their ship is moving through our atmosphere. A similar object on a much larger scale is used to purify the atmosphere within their craft. No space person ever comes to Earth without one of these for protection to help him withstand the radiation present not only in our atmosphere, but in our food and water as well. (…)"[26]

"Their instruments have been developed with minerals and elements from their own planets, therefore contain frequencies harmonious with the users. Protective objects for Earth's people must be constructed from the elements and minerals of our planet in order for them to blend with the frequencies of our bodies in their relationship to Earth. Research is now being conducted in an effort to work out the necessary details for such an instrument." [27]

With regard to crashes, it must be noted that Benjamin Creme insists that UFOs cannot crash. Of the famous crash near Roswell, New Mexico, USA, he has said that it "was not an accident but a deliberate act of sacrifice on the part of each individual in the spaceship. Normally those spaceships cannot crash – they are made of etheric matter, so they have no weight, they cannot be destroyed. The occupants deliberately brought down the vibrational rate of the matter into the dense physical and crashed the spaceship, so that we would have the evidence of the spaceship and five spacemen who could be studied and seen to be certainly similar to humans on this planet, if not identical."[28] Perhaps the crew of the UFOs that were involved in the early crashes did fall ill as a result of exposure to radiation, as Adamski said, but did so on purpose.

In the 2002 documentary *The Secret – Evidence We Are Not Alone*, about the Majestic-12 documents that show the US government has always taken a great interest in the UFO phenomenon, has known far more about it than it is even now admitting and has gone out of its way to keep from the general public, M. Sgt. Frank Kaufmann, of the US Army Intelligence Corps and eyewitness to the craft and the bodies that were recovered from the Roswell crash site, stated: "[The craft] carried no fuel… They assumed it was propelled by the series of cells, octagon-shaped cells, underneath the craft itself, which indicates that evidently they were grafting energy from the atmosphere some way. That is one of the areas that they haven't discovered or haven't found out yet."[29]

Adamski hinted at this source of unlimited, free energy, which the space people use for space travel, when he wrote in *Inside the Space Ships*: "A pillar about two feet thick extended downward from the very top of the dome to the center of the floor. Later I was told that this was the magnetic pole of the ship, by means of which they drew on Nature's forces for propulsion purposes…" The Martian Firkon explains: "The top of the pole is normally positive, while the bottom, which you will notice goes down through the floor, is negative. But, when necessary, these poles can be reversed merely by pushing a button."[30] Later, in 1958, Adamski added: "[T]heir power is drawn from space the same as we draw the breath that keeps our bodies alive. In each case Nature's elements are converted into power or energy.... The visitors, working in harmony with Nature, have learned how to harness this energy; but because of our hostility towards one another, they did not explain the details of their process to me."[31]

The same notion can be found in Orfeo Angelucci's *The Secret of the Saucers*: "...the disks were powered and controlled by tapping into universal magnetic forces; thus their activated molecules received and converted energy inherent in all the universe"[32], while in his book *Unearthly Disclosure* author Timothy Good documents that according to a US Air Force officer, some extraterrestrial craft "use a form of electromagnetic propulsion, taking advantage of the Earth's magnetic field."[33]

However, for interplanetary travel no actual propulsion seems to be necessary. As Adamski was told, "Speed to us does not mean what it does to you. For once a ship is launched into outer space, the speed of the ship is equal to the activity in space! Instead of being artificially propelled, as are your planes, ours travel on the currents of space."[34] With regard to the term 'flying saucers' Adamski is told: "[W]e do not fly as you mean it. We nullify the atmosphere by a mechanical procedure. You express it as 'suspending gravity'... This is why our craft are able to make the sharp changes in direction of travel and to move at the speeds that have so mystified your airmen and your scientists."[35]

This is explained to Enrique Barrios by his space contact as "canceling inertia"[36]. Barrios has Ami saying: "...we do not

Page 107: This photograph, taken near Basel, Switzerland on 19 February 2010, of a 100 meter long cylindrical object does not show the huge dome of about 50 meters height above it, or the bubble shape near the ground that the eye-witnesses saw. According to Benjamin Creme's Master the photograph is a kind of X-ray of the internal structure of a large space ship with the vertical tube-like column showing a technical component of most UFOs, which the crew uses to reverse gravity. It runs

centrally from the dome at the top of the craft to its base, as described by George Adamski. The Master added: "As soon as the 'switch' is thrown, the vehicle is free of the pull of gravity and rises automatically. (...) Some nations, including the US, Britain, Russia and Germany, have been looking for this anti-gravity technology for many years. They have been shown it by the Space Brothers." (*Share International* magazine, March 2011, p.16) Benjamin Creme later added that our scientists have yet to 'grasp' the technology they have been shown.

'travel', rather we 'situate' ourselves" through "the contraction and curvature of space-time" although, about travelling vast distances in space, Benjamin Creme says: "It is not that space and time 'fold together' but actually more simply that time and space at a higher level do not exist; they are an illusion. Those Who are already Masters of Space – the Space Brothers – can travel enormous 'distances', as we think of it, in seconds of 'time'."[37]

The nuclear opt-out

As documented in *George Adamski – A Herald for the Space Brothers*, after the discovery of nuclear fission technology and the nuclear explosions and testing that have been carried out since, the space people have done their utmost to neutralize the radioactivity that has been released in our atmosphere through nuclear tests and nuclear power plants. According to Adamski the radiation would be "be much more pervasive than it is today"[38] without their intervention, while Benjamin Creme, who says that our scientists do not even have the equipment to measure the damage that radiation causes on the etheric planes, calls it "the deadliest release of energy that has ever taken place on Earth", which depletes our body's immune system, "causing more and more Alzheimer's, memory loss, disorientation and the gradual breakdown of our body's defence system".[39]

Apart from the obvious effects that a nuclear war would have in terms of the annihilation of humanity, the poisoning of our soil, water and air that would render the planet barren for countless millennia, the space people said: "It is possible that the body of your planet itself could be mutilated to an extent that would destroy her balance in our galaxy. (...) For us, traveling through space could be made difficult and dangerous for a long time to come, since the energies released in such multiple explosions would then penetrate through your atmosphere into outer space."[40]

The explosion of nuclear devices has caused abnormal conditions within our atmosphere, warn the Space Brothers, which have built up in the ionosphere: "It has continued to grow in depth with each explosion; and little by little is falling back to Earth."[41] According to Benjamin Creme, this buildup of nuclear radiation in the atmosphere, despite the best efforts of the space people to neutralize the effects as much as they are allowed within the Law of Karma, which takes up 90 per cent of their time and effort[42], is flushed out of the atmosphere through torrential rains that are the result of climate change. "These rains not only cause floods but bring down many very toxic pollutants, including nuclear radiation, released into the atmosphere by every nuclear power station", causing the recent mass deaths of birds and fish.[43]

One of the dangerous conditions that arise from nuclear tests, according to Adamski, are concentrations of radiation which at times gather together and under certain circumstances "can extract enough elements from the atmosphere as 'fireballs'. With their finer instruments, space people are able to detect these ... pockets of radiation, visible or invisible; and when they do, they intercept and disintegrate them..."[44]

Similarly, atomic clouds that result from atomic explosions are composed of the same concentrated energy, but on a much larger scale. Adamski explains: "Should one of our planes contact such an invisible 'cloud', it would either explode or disintegrate, seeming to disappear before the eyes of the onlooker. This explains some of the mysterious plane disappearances that have been reported. Since on several occasions space ships were being tracked on radar, and in some instances even visual reports were made of them in the vicinity of a disappearing plane, the implication has been that space ships were kidnapping our planes. But I have been told that because of our inefficient instruments for detection, space people know our pilots are helpless in the path of these 'clouds'. To avoid these very tragedies, they do their utmost to reach the concentrated mass as quickly as possible. However, there have been occasions when they arrived just as one or more of our planes were entering one of these pockets of concentrated energy. Under the circumstances, they were unable to do more than stand by; because once a plane is caught in such a force it is impossible to save either the plane or its occupants. But they then later disintegrate the invisible cloud to avoid further catastrophe."[45] With their more sophisticated instruments the Space Brothers can detect and neutralize these destructive clouds.

Interestingly, in his article 'Binding Forces' Wilbert B. Smith gave a similar reason for a number of unexplained plane crashes. The people from 'elsewhere' informed him "that our pilots flew around in complete disregard of the regions of reduced binding with which this planet is afflicted, and very often their [air]craft were not designed with a sufficient factor of safety and came apart. (...) They also passed a few uncomplimentary remarks about our propensity for shooting off atom bombs which actually created a pair of such 'vortices' with each explosion."[46] Apparently, Smith believed that this is also what caused the mysterious crash of Captain Thomas F. Mantell of the Kentucky Air National Guard in January 1948, that has been blamed on hostile UFO activity.[47]

In June 1958 Adamski gave further information about the dangerous effects of nuclear radiation: "Long before the detonation of the first atomic bomb our scientists were studying the natural cosmic rays coming from space. Their research had proved that under certain conditions these rays could be deadly; but normally their harmful effects were filtered out by their passage through our atmosphere. However, exploding the first nuclear bomb started an artificial barrier against the customary free flow of these rays, and each succeeding detonation has added to its depth until now the cosmic rays must hammer their way through this artificial barrier of radiation. This results in sporadic break-throughs of such high concentrations of cosmic rays, that our atmosphere cannot filter out all the harmful radiation coming to us from space.

"This barrier of radiation of our own making could be compared to a dam with a large body of water behind it. When the first small fissure appears in the dam, the weight of the stored-up water will rush through with unnatural force. The same principle applies to the cosmic rays breaking through the radiation clouds with which we have surrounded the planet at the present time. As a result, our atmosphere is being polluted by these natural forces of space, as well as by the [radioactive fallout from the] nuclear bombs that have been, and are still being, exploded around the world. This is an abnormal condition of our own making ... only we can change it. But were we to ban all future nuclear tests, it still would take years for the atmosphere to clear."[48]

As mentioned in Chapter 1, at a press conference in September 2010 researcher Robert Hastings announced that around 120 former military officials have testified to the fact that UFOs are taking a notable interest in our nuclear capability – which, according to Benjamin Creme, is now shared by twenty-four nations.[49] In 1983, however, Adamski's Swiss contact Lou Zinsstag already suspected that the extraterrestrials seemed "to dislike our use of outer space as proving grounds for military research, especially the growing use of military satellites by both super-powers." In particular, she pointed out, the types of satellites that carry atomic reactors and fuel on board. Specifically, she was referring to the Russian satellite Cosmos 954 that came down in January 1978 in Northern Canada, which she speculates "was sent down by somebody who did not want it to reach a higher orbit". Similarly, an American Skylab came down in January 1979, this time in Australia. When Mrs Zinsstag writes "It looks as if both were refused by somebody…" she reminds her readers that, already in 1963, George Adamski told her about an atomic bomb that the US Air Force had carried high up into the Earth's stratosphere in 1960, where it was exploded for experimental reasons: "The Russians had similar ideas but the Americans wanted to be first. After the first test, however, the whole project was suddenly scrapped and never resumed – on either side. 'The warning was very clear,' Adamski said, 'because a strong voice was calling out 'Negative! Negative! Negative!' And so it was the plan for the test series which exploded, but not the bomb!'"[50]

Benjamin Creme's information is that the Space Brothers are engaged on a spiritual mission to neutralize this nuclear radiation, which confirms Alberto Perego's statements to the same effect (see page 56). In fact, his Master has said: "Life on this planet would be utter misery were it not for the help of our Space Brothers who neutralize this pollution and render it harmless within karmic limits. Fleets of their space ships, using implosion devices, do this on a daily basis."[51]

At the same time they are replicating the planet's magnetic field on the dense-physical plane, as part of a new energy grid that will "give this planet … unlimited, safe power for all purposes, in ways that cannot be bought up or cornered by any group of men."[52] Crop circles, says Creme, are found in locations where the Earth's magnetic lines intercept and vortices of

The blinding blue light that was filmed near Tokyo on 7 april 2011, during the 7.5 earthquake there, was the result of space ships counteracting the energy of the earthquake by causing it to 'implode'. According to Benjamin Creme's Master, the "implosion" technology which the Space Brothers have been using to neutralize concentrations of radioactive pollution, is now also being developed to mitigate the effects of earthquakes. (*Share International* magazine, May 2011, p.11)

magnetic energy exist which are used in this way by the space people. The space people use crop circles as a "tangential way, without infringing our free will, of telling the people of Earth that [they] are here, are part of our [solar] system and that they work in a systematic way, not just as separate planets. They are helping this planet to develop the technology of the future, and also to make known, quietly, that they are 100 per cent friendly and harmless."[53] As for the crop circles, Creme says that a minority of only around 4 per cent are hoaxes, while the rest are authentic.[54] Where there are no crops, there are usually no traces of this particular activity of the space people, although increasingly, it seems, similar circles are being found in snow and bodies of water that are frozen over.

Through their technology, the space people are establishing the foundation of what Creme calls the Technology of Light, in which energy direct from the sun will be combined with energy from the Earth's magnetic field. Through the Technology of Light this energy, which is available in every location around the world, will be stored in boxes of various shapes and sizes, depending on their use for industrial or domestic purposes, and be available for free in limitless quantities. Benjamin Creme's Master has said in an interview: "This will provide the energy for all human needs. It will be clean, without waste, and there will be an inexhaustible supply to every home in every city in the world. Help is being given to scientists in Russia and in the United States by our Space Brothers."[55]

A possible example of this was described by Bruno Sammaciccia when he was shown around an underground base near Forlimpopoli, Italy. The extraterrestrial Meredir showed him a device which he said was very different from any electronic devices that we know and contained an energy load that would suffice them for a whole year: "He opened its cover, and inside there was a screen, and over it a wide light was moving, without making any noise; it was a light, a dark green one, but it was as if there was some matter in it, maybe one could even touch it. It was like a boiling broth. 'This is energy at its initial state. It may be transformed into solid energy, or into even more subtle energy. And this depends on this small instrument nearby. (...) You see, if you touch that knob in some point, it will select the kind and the amount of energy you require, then it will distribute it wherever you like, inside this base.' "[56]

And according to Benjamin Creme (in 1991), "There is a town in the Soviet Union whose energy sources are all received directly from the sun through one of their satellites. That is the use of Light Technology. This technology is more advanced in the Soviet Union than elsewhere because the Space Brothers have had a base there for the last 15 years."[57]

Sharing technology
In his book *Light at the End of the Tunnel – A Survival Plan for the Human Species* Paul Hellyer discards the outcome of the Copenhagen climate summit in 2009 as ineffective, while demanding disclosure of the available extraterrestrial technology to help in the transition towards clean and safe energy, saying: "There is no doubt in my mind that the Star Visitors would give us the technology necessary to save the planet if we asked them to."[58] Decades earlier, Wilbert Smith stated categorically that the space people "stand by ready and willing to render [their] help. In fact, they have already helped us a great deal, along the lines that do not interfere with our freedom of choice."[59]

Descriptions in documents that are linked to the Majestic-12 Special Studies Group indeed seem to indicate that the space people have not been shy to share their technology, which has helped humanity make tremendous strides in technological achievement over the last 50 to 60 years. In the documentary *The Secret – Evidence We are Not Alone*, mathematician and computer scientist Ryan S. Wood, who is also one of the main MJ-12 researchers, refers to an analytical report from the Research and Development Laboratory which discusses extraterrestrial technology: "Flight instruments and controls are activated by optical wave guide fibers similar to glass rods except they are flexible and have a plastic cladding wrap. All functions may be operated by touch sensitive or texture sensing stimuli. Instruments are covered by a plastic plate and seem to be color coded."[60] Not only does this amount, as Mr Wood points out, to a description of fibre-optics technology in 1947, but also of touchscreen technology that has only become commonplace since the introduction of smart phones in 2007 and tablet computers in 2010.

Another document, prepared and approved by Lt General Nathan Twining in the late summer of 1947, included the results of what government scientists and engineers had been able to evaluate and determine of saucer technology during that summer and describes "a series of fine grid-like lines connecting a series of dots of pure silver, which is highly reminiscent of what we know now as integrated circuits, or computer chips."[61]

According to Benjamin Creme, "It is true that [the Space Brothers] are working to some extent with scientists in America and Russia. They are both impressing their minds and working with them in the laboratory."[62] He described one example of a technology that has been developed with the co-operation of the extraterrestrials, "that can monitor every movement on Earth…"[63], which apparently was the reason behind the Russians' and the Americans' calls for major disarmament in the 1980s.

One example, Creme has confirmed, of a scientist who has worked alongside the Space Brothers was Dr Michael Wolf (1941-2000), who wrote about his experiences in his book *The Catchers of Heaven*, although he was only allowed to publish it on the condition that it was fictionalized. This, of course, makes it difficult to separate fact from fiction in his book, both with regard to his personal life and his scientific work for the US government, which must be one reason why his claims and revelations are considered controversial. It makes it most likely that he doesn't refer to any officials by their real names, and neither do we know if the diary of his son from which he quotes at length is not just a narrative device to express his own thoughts and philosophies.

Dr Wolf (real name Michael Wulf Kruvant) wrote his book in the memory of his wife Sarah and teenage son Daniel, who died when he drove his car off a cliff in Switzerland during their Christmas holiday in 1984.[64] In the book he seems to imply that foul play was involved, but he doesn't go beyond that. After having originally vouchsafed the truth of Dr Wolf's story in the 1990s, his brother Ron Kruvant came out in an interview in 2008 to say that Michael had had mental problems and made up most of the story in his book. However, in 2010 Hong Kong-based researcher Neil Gould interviewed French electronics engineer and intelligence officer Philippe de la Mezussière, who confirmed that Dr Wolf had met and worked with extra-terrestrials for five years. At one time, Mr De la Mezussière states, he was in a room with Dr Wolf when two space people entered for a few minutes, who were working with Dr Wolf on the same project.[65]

While *The Catchers of Heaven* (1993), with Dr Wolf's long spun-out mourning and yearning for his deceased wife and son, interwoven with his experiences and philosophical musings, is

not an easy read, it does provide various interesting corroborations of statements that can also be found in the reports of other
contactees. Wolf says, for instance: "We must realize that we are
not alone in this vast universe, that we have cosmic neighbors
who cannot stand for beauty to be deliberately destroyed for
wealth and personal power, things that OFFWORLDERS have most
probably already passed beyond in their evolution." Likewise,
his description of the interior of a saucer is strongly reminiscent
of what we read before in the descriptions of Adamski, Angelucci
and Dibitonto: "We were standing in what seemed to me as a
very familiar room, brilliantly lit, but not as much as to hurt the
eyes. The light seemed not to emanate from any single source, but
was everywhere. The doorway that closed appeared not to have
any juncture or architectural connection or seams or handle."[66]

His concept of space and propulsion also rings familiar: "In
a hyperspace environment, using shipboard generation of
amplified gravity waves, *it isn't that speed increases; it is that linear
time, when acted upon by a force (i.e. gravity), reduces itself,* so that
one might say, space-time is 'warped'. (...) In such advanced
gravity manipulation, space itself is not transversed or physically
crossed; space folds in on itself as gravity waves act upon time
(...) thus a spacecraft has little difficulty getting from point A to
point B without the so-called 'normal' concept of propulsion."[67]

At the same time, the space people had no problems
utilizing 'old-fashioned' Earth technology such as radio and
audio tape recorders to communicate with their Italian contacts
as we saw in Chapter 4.

The space people not only employed radio frequencies for
their communication in the South American branch of their
Friendship efforts. Bruno Sammaciccia writes that the people
in the Italian Friendship group also received regular communications without using the wireless. Breccia writes: "Once, at

Bruno's, I got a message from a transistor set (it wasn't a radio, but a portable disk player, therefore without a tuning section); first I cut the power cable, then I opened it and cut one of the loudspeaker cables, and nothing changed! The loudspeaker was going on, as if everything was OK."[68]

An interesting correlation can be found in an article about extraterrestrial 'recording devices' by Robert Caswell in the December 1967 issue of *UFO Contact*, the Danish-British co-publication of George Adamski's international Get Acquainted Program. He relates how Wilbert Smith, the Canadian government engineer, UFO researcher and contactee, carried out part of his correspondence by recording 'letters' on audio tape. On one occasion, while recording a letter to an engineer, himself a contactee, Smith "inadvertently allowed scientific information received by him from his extraterrestrial sources via contactees to go on to tape. He had forgotten that, for the time being, the information was to remain confidential." When, some time later, the tape was returned to him by the correspondent who didn't know what it was about, and Smith played back the tape, he was amazed to find "certain blank spaces, slightly sticky to the touch, which he knew had not been left blank during the taping session. He realized with some sense of shock that the 'blank' spaces were those areas on which the special, confidential information had been recorded. They had been wiped clean!"[69]

As we saw in Chapter 2, many of the misconceptions about the UFO phenomenon and related conspiracy theories are rooted in facts that have been misunderstood or twisted. A similar situation seems to pertain to the issue of implants. For instance, Bruno Sammaciccia tells of a technological enhancement through which communication with the space people was facilitated.

One day, while walking on the beach, they told him to send his dog Dik, a German shepherd, into the sea. "[A]ll of a sudden, it looked at me and made a strange sound…" The space people then informed Sammaciccia that they had placed 'nuclei' in the dog's pads, which were electrically oscillating negative and positive poles. They assured Bruno that it didn't hurt the dog at all, but apparently it did help communications: "When we had to get in touch with them, we usually arranged ourselves in a circle, with Dik in the middle. The dog was usually lying down, and as the communication began, I felt the process happening much easier than before…"[70] Until that time, the

Bruno Sammaciccia (left), with Gaspare de Lama, and Bruno's German shepherd dog Dik, that served as an 'amplifier' after the friends from space had implanted 'nuclei' in its paws to facilitate communications.

friends had to come within 30 kilometers of a certain location that had been especially prepared for the purpose of communicating with the space visitors, for which they were also asked to wear copper plates in their shoes, or carry "a small, rectangular plate whose color was between platinum, and silver, with a lot of, say, small diamonds all over its surface", which the space people had given them and which they had to wrap in a sheet of aluminium foil.[71]

Technology and awareness

According to Benjamin Creme, "Technology is the result of human creativity. Every evolutionary advance has been accompanied by a technological one. Our present technology (…) is, from the esoteric standpoint, Atlantean magic on a higher turn on the spiral."[72] This statement is especially poignant in light of H.P. Blavatsky's explanation of the word 'magic', which she says, "means, in its spiritual sense, the 'Great Life,' or divine life in *spirit*. The root is *magh*, as seen in the Sanskrit *mahat*, Zend *maz*, Greek *megas* and Latin *magus*, all signifying 'great'."[73]

So with growth of consciousness comes greater creativity that expresses itself in every civilization as technological advances. However, if this is not also accompanied by a greater understanding of life and a heightened sense of responsibility, and the focus remains solely on the material or physical aspect of life, with the moral and ethical development lagging behind, the integrity of our society and indeed our planetary life is at stake, as we can see in the rapidly deteriorating physical condition of the planet – with our very habitat being squandered, pillaged and plundered for profit.

On several occasions the space people have warned us of the risks of putting technology over spirituality, for instance through

Bruno Sammaciccia: "[By] many other peoples, technology and science are held as the most important things, so that they forget people are souls, above all; if [man] forgets this simple concept, he is going to face serious risks (...) Unfortunately, you are going this way, and you are going to face serious problems in your near future. Moreover, there is also another problem with you: money. You could solve many of your environmental difficulties, but the great economic powers prevent such solutions from being adopted."[74]

A similar message was given to Enrique Barrios, who related it as follows: "When the scientific level overwhelms the level of love in a world, that world self-destructs. There is a mathematical relationship..."[75]

Other contactees, too, were told the same thing. Orfeo Angelucci's contacts, for instance, informed him: "Already man's material knowledge has far outstripped the growth of brotherly love and spiritual understanding in his heart. Therein lies the present danger. To add to the destructive phase of man's scientific knowledge is not permitted. We are working now to turn that knowledge to constructive purposes upon Earth. Also we hope to give men a deeper knowledge and understanding of their own true nature and a greater awareness of the evolutionary crisis facing them."[76] And, during his visit to a Saturnian mother ship, Adamski was told: "Now that your scientific knowledge has so far outstripped your social and human progress, the gap between *must* be filled with urgent haste."[77]

In order to do that, the Space Brothers did not just initiate attempts to teach humanity how to express our innate spirituality through harmlessness in our relations, as per Adamski's GAP and the Friendship efforts, but they have shared their technology in so far as that is safe in the hands of a race that has not yet abandoned war as an approach to settling conflicts. Some examples of these have been described above.

With regard to the acquisition of extraterrestrial technology former astronaut Dr Edgar Mitchell has said: "I suspect some of [the UFO craft] are home-grown, I suspect that in the last 60 years or so there has been some back-engineering, and the creation of this type of equipment, but it is not nearly as sophisticated yet as what the apparent visitors have."[78] His suspicion is confirmed by esotericist Benjamin Creme, who says that while a number of governments, notably the American, Russian and some others, have managed to back-engineer some degree of 'anti-gravity' technology, none of them have "achieved the complete control of space, appearing and disappearing at will, travelling at momentous speeds etc, as is demonstrated by our Space Brothers. These functions are only possible by the Space Brothers because the vehicles are not made of what we call solid physical matter."[79]

George Adamski used to point out to his audiences that "Within the many phases of Nature can be found a blueprint for any mechanical devise. The space people merely used the basic laws governing their planet for constructing their ships." Although Earth is orbiting the sun at a speed of 162 miles per second, while revolving on its axis at approximately 18,5 miles per second, Adamski explains, "...we feel no sense of motion, nor do we experience gravitational difficulties; because we are protected by the atmosphere encompassing this giant globe. But this atmosphere is created by the Earth's movement through space!" Having analyzed this situation carefully, he said, the space people "incorporated into their craft a mechanical means of artificially creating a protective force field, or 'atmosphere' around their ships."[80]

Moreover, says Benjamin Creme, in confirmation of Adamski's statement: "Spaceships cannot be shot down by our weapons because each ship has around it a magnetic field which rejects every weapon; it can put weapons off course. The spaceships are impenetrable. They are literally invulnerable; however, several times in the past the Space People have sacrificed themselves in a simulated crash of their vehicle such as the Roswell incident. This is a measure of the extraordinary love which is behind their work for humanity. It is truly a spiritual mission – even to the point of self-sacrifice carried out in a way which I don't think this planet would be able to repeat."[81] Research shows that there have been at least three confirmed UFO crashes in the US alone, i.e. Cape Girardeau, Missouri in 1941, San Antonio, New Mexico in 1945, and Roswell, New Mexico in 1947, with reports of further crashes in San Bernardino, California in 1942 and near Albuquerque, New Mexico in 1963, plus several reports from Russia, Brasil and Puerto Rico.

As to the construction of the space ships, Orfeo Angelucci said that "…the complexities of the apparently simple structure of their disks were so great that to an Earthling a saucer would be considered as having 'synthetic brains', although each one is to a degree under the remote control of a Mother Ship."[82]

Dr Michael Wolf seemed to be referring to such synthetic brains when he said that "…there are LIVING CONVEYANCES … I have seen the so-called pieces of metal that radiate energy, energy which 'seems' to behave intelligently."[83] Another reference is made in his book by a 3-star general whom he calls Lieutenant General Robert Lewis: "And now we don't want to know that even our most advanced technology is primitive at best when compared to extraterran science – the 'New Physics' – and their mental merging or interfacing with and into it, allowing, at times, little, if any, reliance on physical instrumentalities."[84]

Also, according to Dr Wolf, "The propagation of gravity and anti-gravity waves *sacrifices no power*. There is power for other 'living' devices, such as 'seamless' doorways [another characteristic found in the descriptions of several contactees], the manipulation of metal (made with cold fusion) and containing what we cannot but call 'living' matter, intelligent matter, so that the seamless doors function with intelligent interfacing, and the size and shape of the CONVEYANCE may be altered to suit the needs of the moment."[85]

Bruno Sammaciccia seems to refer to this "living matter" when he writes: "Their suits are living entities, that adapt themselves to the body they cover", to the point that they apparently cannot be worn by others.[86] His notion, in turn, seems to be confirmed in a statement made by researcher William Brophy, whose father was a B-29 bomber pilot based at Alamogordo AAF in New Mexico, USA and was involved with the recovery of the UFO that had crashed near San Antonio, New Mexico, on 15 August 1945. Mr Brophy states: "The scientists at Wright Patterson AFB who tested the special memory material suits that the 1945 San Antonio aliens wore, were receiving memories of flying in UFOs..." He also said: "The suits are kept in a separate vault as the USAF considers them living memory material."[87]

With their knowledge of the use and control over energies of the universe, according to the Master from Venus in Adamski's *Inside the Space Ships*, "we could, if we wished, nullify your force with our greater force."[88] In fact, Adamski added later, "When we realize that an instrument no larger than a cigarette package, in the hands of an unscrupulous person, could with this power destroy a form without leaving a trace, we can understand their hesitancy in sharing such knowledge with us."[89] However, the Master reassured Adamski, "We do not kill our fellow man, even in self-defense."[90] Michael Wolf, too, indicates as much, when he says: "I think it must be quite a problem (…), when a general who really enjoys his power wakes up one day to find that he has no real power at all, that there are extraterran visitors who, with the movement of a finger, or the thinking of a thought to action, could neutralize and invalidate any power on earth."[91]

Likewise, Meredir told Bruno Sammaciccia about a group of young extraterrestrial scientists in training: "…we take care much more of moral aspects, because they get in touch with powerful weapons, and if they were not provided with a strong ethical attitude, they could cause great damage. This same ethical attitude we have imposed to our instruments, even to our weapons; if you would try to use them to do harm, they would not work, or they would even disintegrate themselves."[92] Bruno Sammaciccia explains this attitude of the space people: "They put their morals before their technology, while here we do just the opposite."[93]

While helping humanity to make significant strides in technological advancement, the space people have not just 'given' us what we wanted to know. They have given hints, shown our scientists samples of their technology for them to work out the principles underlying it, or impressed their minds with solutions to existing technological limitations. This way, any new development still requires a major effort of understanding on our part for, as the editors of *Topside*, the publication of the Ottawa New Sciences Club that was founded by Wilbert Smith, stated in 1969: "…it is against the Cosmic Laws of the Space Brothers to drop *unearned* answers to scientific questions into the laps of Earth scientists…", adding that "… all that WBS received from them were certain guidelines or suggested avenues of research for him to explore and the actual work of finding the answers to scientific problems was left to WBS to fathom out."[94]

Much of their technology arises from a deep understanding of the underlying oneness and interconnectedness of everything in Cosmos, without which understanding the necessary breakthroughs in development or employment of technologies such as used in their anti-gravity devices will elude us. It is for that reason that Benjamin Creme says the Technology of Light will only be given to humanity, "when we have relinquished war and all the horrors of our modern economic and political systems."[95]

Only when we have made a breakthrough in our perception of Life and ourselves as being essentially One and intimately interrelated, and when we understand that the physical-plane expression of that Life is not a haphazard occurrence for us to tamper with at will, but an integral part of that Whole, can we be trusted with the technology, science and energies that derive directly from the heart of creation. Hence, Adamski has said: "We have much growing to do before it will be safe for us to be given a full understanding of the natural forces that they have harnessed for propelling their ships. For this same energy can be perverted for terrible destruction as easily as it can be used for the progress of mankind."[96]

Notes

1 Stefano Breccia (2009), *Mass Contacts*, pp.284-85
2 Ibidem, p.187
3 Paola Harris (2006), 'Why Me?'. Interview with Maurizio Cavallo [online]. Available at <www.paolaharris.com/cavallo.htm> [Accessed 19 August 2011]
4 See Benjamin Creme's comment about the photograph of space people, seen in the etheric, exiting an underground basis in Ongamira, Argentina, in Chapter 4.
5 See e.g. Rupert Sheldrake (1981), *A New Science of Life – The Hypothesis of Formative Causation*

6 Giorgio Dibitonto (1990), *Angels in Starships*, p.42
7 Wilhelm Reich (1942), 'The Discovery of the Orgone'. In Wilhelm Reich (1960), *Selected Writings*, p.195
8 Creme (2010), *The Gathering of the Forces of Light – UFOs and their Spiritual Mission*, p.67
9 Enrique Barrios (1989), *Ami, Child of the Stars*, p.42
10 Gerard Aartsen (2010), *George Adamski – A Herald for the Space Brothers*, pp.7-8
11 George Adamski (1957-58), *Cosmic Science for the Promotion of Cosmic Principles and Truths*, Part 1, Question #12
12 Desmond Leslie & George Adamski (1970), *Flying Saucers Have Landed*, Revised and Enlarged edition, p.250
13 Timothy Good (1998), *Alien Base – Earth's Encounters with Extraterrestrials*, p.152
14 Creme (2001), *The Great Approach – New Light and Life for Humanity*, p.133
15 Creme (2010), op cit, p.49
16 Dibitonto (1990), op cit, p.82
17 Creme (2010), op cit, p.57
18 Adamski (1957-58), op cit, Part 4, Question #67
19 Orfeo Angelucci (1955), *The Secret of the Saucers*, p.20-21
20 Dibitonto (1990), op cit, p.67
21 Adamski (1955), *Inside the Space Ships*, p.50
22 Ibid., p.119
23 Adamski (1957-58), op cit, Part 3, Question #46
24 Adamski (1955), op cit, p.150
25 Alberto Perego (1958), *Sono Extraterrestri!*, 20th and 21st page in photo section (unnumbered)

Space travel
26 Adamski (1957-58), op cit, Part 1, Question #7
27 Ibid., Part 1, Question #8
28 Creme (2001), op cit, pp.133-34
29 Laurent Basset (dir.; 2002), *The Secret – Evidence We Are Not Alone.*
30 Adamski (1955), op cit, p.47
31 Adamski (1957-58), op cit, Part 5, Question #82
32 Angelucci (1955), op cit, p.10
33 Good (2000), *Unearthly Disclosure*, p.262
34 Adamski (1955), op cit, p.70
35 Ibid., p.89
36 Barrios (1989), op cit, p.46
37 Creme (2010), op cit, p.59

The nuclear opt-out

38 Adamski (1957-58), op cit, Part 2, Question #26
39 Creme (2010), op cit, p.13-14
40 Adamski (1955), op cit, p.92
41 Adamski (1957-58), op cit, Part 4, Question #73
42 Creme (ed.; 2011), *Share International* magazine, Vol.30, No.6, July/August, p.18
43 Creme (ed.; 2011), op cit, Vol.30, No.3, April, p.27
44 Adamski (1957-58), op cit, Part 2, Question #27
45 Ibid., Part 2, Question #28
46 Wilbert B. Smith (1961), 'Binding Forces'. *Flying Saucer Review*, Vol.7, No.2, March-April, p.7
47 Smith (1958), speech given 31 March in Ottowa, Canada. Transcript published in *Flying Saucer Review* Vol.9, No.5, September-October 1963, pp.14-15
48 Adamski (1957-58), op cit, Part 4, Question #73
49 Creme (2010), op cit, p.71
50 Lou Zinsstag & Timothy Good (1983), *George Adamski – The Untold Story*, pp.94-95
51 Creme (1997), *Maitreya's Mission Vol.3*, p.192
52 Creme (2010), op cit, p.15
53 Ibid., p.186
54 Ibid., p.187
55 Creme (1997), op cit, p.194
56 Breccia (2009), op cit, p.190-91
57 Creme (1993), *Maitreya's Mission Vol.2*, p.199

Sharing technology

58 Paul Hellyer (2010), *Light at the End of the Tunnel – A Survival Plan for the Human Species*, pp.242-43
59 Smith (n.d.; 1950s), 'The Philosophy of the Saucers'. Available at <www.presidentialufo.com/wilbert-smith-articles/125-the-philosophy-of-the-saucers> [Accessed 28 March 2011]
60 Basset (dir.; 2002), op cit.
61 Ibid.
62 Creme (2010), op cit, p.68
63 See for instance Creme (1993), op cit, p.197
64 Michael Wolf (1993), *The Catchers of Heaven*, 1996 reprint, p.114
65 Neil Gould (2010), interview with Philippe de la Mezussière, [online] July. Available at <www.youtube.com/watch?v=yOR1NNg90c0>
66 Wolf (1993), op cit, p.199
67 Ibid., pp.254-55
68 Breccia (2009), op cit, p.250

69 Ronald Caswell (1967), 'Wired for sound'. *UFO Contact*, IGAP journal vol.2, no.8, December, p.213
70 Breccia (2009), op cit, p.175
71 Ibid., p.174

Technology and awareness
72 Creme (ed.; 2011), op cit, Vol.30, No.4, May, p.23
73 H.P. Blavatsky (1897), *The Secret Doctrine* Vol.III, 6th Adyar ed., 1971, vol.5, footnote p.444
74 Breccia (2009), op cit, pp.244-45
75 Barrios (1989), op cit, p.20
76 Angelucci (1955), op cit, p.33
77 Adamski (1955), op cit, p.137
78 Interview with Dr Edgar Mitchell in Nick Margerrison (2008), Kerrang! Radio, UK, 23 July. Available at <www.youtube.com/watch?v=RhNdxdveK7c>
79 Creme (ed.; 2011), op cit, Vol.30, No.8, October, p.22
80 Adamski (1957-58), op cit, Part 3, Question #47
81 Creme (ed.; 2010a), *Share International* Vol.29, No.8, October, p.23
82 Angelucci (1955), op cit, p.10
83 Wolf (1993), op cit, p.110
84 Ibid., p.316
85 Ibid., p.213
86 Breccia (2009), op cit, p.230
87 William Brophy (2011), comment on Facebook posting, [online] 18 September. Available at <www.facebook.com/groups/EWNEUSN/>
88 Adamski (1955), op cit, p.92
89 Adamski (1957-58), op cit, Part 5, Question #82
90 Adamski (1955), op cit, p.92
91 Wolf (1993), op cit, p.323
92 Breccia (2009), op cit, p.189
93 Ibid, p.192
94 The Editors of TOPSIDE (1969), 'The Space Brothers' Philosophy – and Wilbert B. Smith'. In Smith (1969), *The Boys from Topside*, pp.11-12
95 Creme (2010), op cit, p.184
96 Adamski (1957-58), op cit, Part 2, Question #23

6. Disclosure: all goes to Plan

If meetings with extraterrestrials, or space people, are always of a positive nature, if they do not abduct, but invite people on board their craft, and if it is not for nasty experiments, is there then no truth at all in the stories about 'negative' ETs?

To be sure, George Adamski's space contacts confirmed that people who "through greed will desire to assume power over other men"[1] can also be found on other worlds. And according to Lou Zinsstag, Adamski also said that in our system "there are three planets which are not friendly to us".[2] In his bulletin of December 1963, Adamski elaborated on this statement when he said: "Recently there have been some Venusian ships attacked by hostile space travelers. But by using the repelling ray, which is a part of the equipment of their ships, the ships of the hostile ones were damaged without destroying life."[3] At the same time, however, he made it quite clear elsewhere that, "[t]here are no monsters that we know about and most of the hostile reports have come from frightened people who in some cases have even shot at them when they came close enough. In cases like this the space people have used a ray to frighten them away, but never to hurt them physically."[4] In fact, the space people that invited Bruno Sammaciccia and his friends into their underground bases told them, when they asked to see young extraterrestrials studying there: "Yes, but secretly; we do not want to frighten them, because what they know about terrestrials is not good news. They think of you as some kind of wild beasts."[5]

Nevertheless, Sammaciccia mentions a group of 'contrarian' extraterrestrials, the so-called CTR, who are less concerned with humanity's welfare than with their own, and who seemed to be competing with the group that the Italian contactees called the 'W56' (see Chapter 4). According to Sammaciccia, the CTR "adore science only, therefore they are very [cold-hearted]... They have a kind of 'scientific ethic'." In an interview in May 2010 Amicizia participant Gaspare de Lama says of the CTR: "This doesn't mean that CTR are bad; if they didn't destroy their own civilisation it means that they love each other, they love their wives, their pets, but they have ideologies that are cooler and straight, science could be their God. While for the W56, God is Love."[6] And, according to Mr Sammaciccia, "they do not abduct people; this phenomenon that today gets so large an echo in UFO books cannot be charged to them." About the war that he says was going on between their contacts from space and the CTR, he expressed the hope that "before leaving, our friends will have arranged things so that the CTR will not be able to trouble us..."[7]

Dr Michael Wolf quotes his extraterrestrial colleague Kolta as saying: "We believe that evil has no proprietary place in this universe, even though it wasn't exclusively found on just one planet. It is truly difficult to understand why beings *invent* and personify evil, when the only true demons were the ones running freely around in a being's own heart, until one sees the wisdom of purging them."[8]

Adamski, like many others, was told that the inhabitants of other worlds are not fundamentally different from Earth humanity: "The purpose of life on other worlds is basically the same as yours. Inherent in all mankind, however deeply buried it may be, is the yearning to rise to something higher. Your school system on Earth is, in a sense, patterned after the universal progress of life. For in your schools you progress from grade to grade and from school to school, toward a higher and fuller education. In the same way, man progresses from planet to planet, and from system to system toward an ever higher understanding and evolvement in universal growth and service."[9] Elsewhere Adamski added: "The Cosmos is a vast school with many departments of learning for every state of being. There are primary planets and planets advanced far beyond the scope of our earthly imaginations."[10]

Thus it is that Enrique Barrios' space contact says, through his character Ami: "There are worlds where you couldn't survive even half an hour... There are worlds inhabited by truly monstrous humans..."[11] And esotericist Benjamin Creme explains that people "do not know how the planet [i.e. Earth] is threatened from negative forces in our own and other, lower planets. These stimulate the negativity of the Earth."[12] In fact, he has even said that the people from Pluto are beings "you would not like to meet on a dark night!"[13]

Law and order

However, this does not mean that just anyone can come to our planet and ransack the place. According to Benjamin Creme "[a]ll Hierarchies of all the planets in this system are in touch wih each other, and everything that takes place in an extra-terrestrial sense takes place under Law."[14] Indeed, he says, all planets are "teeming with life at different stages. We are at a midway stage; Venus is unbelievably evolved compared with this planet, as is Jupiter, Mercury, Saturn and various other planets. They have no *need* to carry out experiments on us; they *know*."[15] What's more, "[t]here is indeed a kind of

Interplanetary Parliament representing all the planets. The Space Brothers are here to help the people of Earth to overcome the difficulties which our own ignorance has brought about, and to work with [the World Teacher], and our Spiritual Hierarchy [of Masters] as a whole, in the work of salvage."[16]

Likewise, of the space travellers George Adamski said: "On Earth we have people of various sizes and colors; this same condition exists in other worlds. (...) Space travelers are identical to us, only they have a deeper understanding of themselves and the Cosmos of which we are all inhabitants. When we, too, learn to master space travel, our concept of the Cosmos will be infinitely broadened."[17]

This notion is corroborated by Bruno Sammaciccia, who was told: "There are other people besides us, at various levels of civilization, but man is universal; you may find small variatons from one race to the next, even among ourselves you have seen very tall persons (...) and very small ones; there may be differences in the skin colour, there are people whose flesh is almost transparant, but, I repeat, almost every civilization is made up of man... A race, whatever race, never gets modified if not by an accident, and when this happens usually the mutation is a degenerative one."[18]

In an exchange between Enrique Barrios' characters Pete asks his extraterrestrial friend Ami if it is not possible that somewhere on any of the millions of worlds an evil race might have survived without destroying themselves before mastering space travel. Ami explains that such beings could never attain the technological advancement necessary to leave their planets in order to invade others: "[I]f a civilization has no kindness and manages to attain a high scientific level, sooner or later it will use its destructive power against itself, long before it can leave for other worlds. (...)

"The monsters we imagine are inside ourselves. Until we abandon them, we cannot attain the wonder of the universe. True intelligence, kindness and love go hand in hand, they are the result of the same evolutionary process toward love." Ami goes so far as to call it a law that no-one can escape.[19]

That such a "law" exists may be easier to understand when we first gain a better understanding of the true nature of life. In his little-known first book *Wisdom of the Masters of the Far East*, in which George Adamski published a summary of the Wisdom teachings that he received when he studied with the Masters in Tibet as a teenager, he states that consciousness is the aspect which moulds all the visible forms from the invisible essence, "first in the invisible state and then gradually bringing it into a state of greater density through a descension [sic] of vibration in the composing elements until it is finally brought into the extreme coarse state of vibration known as visible manifestation."[20] From there, the teachings tell us, the evolution of form begins, to facilitate the evolution of consciousness as the ever expanding expression of Life according to a Plan.

As a result of this process of evolution, there are Hierarchies of Masters on all the planets, who serve the Plan of their particular Planetary Logos. Together, the Planetary Logoi form the various centres of a solar system, similar to the chakras in our etheric body, as the body of expression of that Solar Logos, and they serve His Plan. When there seem to be 'orphan planets' such as that were recently discovered seemingly floating freely through our galaxy instead of orbiting around stars, according to Benjamin Creme these are "the physical planets of a solar system whose sun has advanced to the etheric physical state and therefore at present is invisible to our sight. In our system the planet Vulcan has reached that same etheric state, so is also invisible to our sight."[21]

However, there is an "eternal struggle that goes on in every solar system between planets at different stages of evolution"[22], says Creme, who asserts that the contacts made on our planet are governed by law: "There was a time when quite dark entities from planets which we might think are very advanced, could come here on their own volition. They did contact quite a lot of people and this went on for some time. *This has been stopped.*"[23] [Emphasis added]

A tantalizingly vivid description of the reality of the Heavenly Being that ensouls our solar system was given by artist and author Vera Stanley Alder, who was a student of the Ageless Wisdom in the group around Alice A. Bailey. The members of this group received personal instructions from the Tibetan Master Djwhal Khul[24] and, based on her studies, Mrs Alder herself wrote six books in which she provided a simplified outline of the teachings of the Master DK through Alice Bailey, while in her last book, which was an autobiography, she shared some of the profound experiences that she was given in 1942 about the nature of Life.

In a series of seven 'lessons' Mrs Alder was taught first how to consciously leave the physical body and, once outside the confines of her solid physical vehicle, experienced how life and consciousness express itself at various of its endless levels of existence, such as the cell in a human body, and even an atom within that cell, but also of humanity as an integral part, or a unit, in the life of the planet, and how discord among the various constituent individual parts affects the well-being of the totality. As George Adamski was told, and himself taught, on numerous occasions, "each individual is a radiating center of influence whose ultimate circumference no one can accurately perceive."[25]

While a fascinating run-down of scientific experiments

with regard to the seemingly conscious response of minerals and plants to external stimuli was given by Yogi Ramacharaka in his book *Lessons in Gnani Yoga – The Yoga of Wisdom* (1909)[26], which might as well have been subtitled 'Wisdom for beginners', in recent years several experiments have provided further evidence that consciousness comes in different gradations and is not unique to the animal and human kingdoms. Dr Masaru Emoto, for instance, conducted experiments which show a definite response in water crystals to written and spoken words.[27] About Dr Emoto's work Benjamin Creme has said that the positive or negative effects lie in both the sound and the intention of the thoughts and emotions behind the words, which affect everything around us through vibration, because "[t]he atoms of all things are inter-connected".[28] Dr Emoto's findings are supported by German resonance researcher and photographer Alexander Lauterwasser, who researched the response of water to the vibration of sounds.[29]

Enrique Barrios is told very much the same thing through his character Ami, who says: "Planets are living beings. (...) Everything is interdependent and interrelated. What happens to Earth affects all the people who inhabit it and what happens to the people affects the Earth."[30]

In one of her 'lessons' in 1942, Mrs Alder is given a glimpse of planet Earth as a living Being, which in turn is only one of the centres in the great Being who constitutes the solar system. First she and her tutor move up high enough to see the Earth's etheric body, which she describes as "an infinitely delicate silver tracery lying over the earth like a cobweb on an autumn morning", and which later is still visible "like a blue phosphorescent light" edging the planet's round surface. Moving up further, they observed the Earth's astral vehicle: "There hung the Earth growing rapidly smaller to our view, poised in the centre of a big beautiful iridescent bubble... Exquisite colours chased each other through and through this mysterious sphere, round and round upon its surface, intermingling with rapid wave-like movements", reflecting the well-being of the Earth, or lack thereof, in response to the changing emotional state of humanity, similar to how the colours in the aura of a human being change or oscillate to reflect our state of being.

In the next stage of the experience, the etheric web of the solar system is observed, which looks like "a fine pulsating web of living electric strands... The Sun was the heart and centre of the cobweb, the very nucleus of it. For I saw that glowing filaments, tinted in the colours of the rainbow, spread out from its heart and linked up with the planets. I counted seven of these living rays, and was thus able to locate the seven major planets. I saw that they ... were nourished and fed with the essence of life by the Sun itself.

"Each planet in its turn radiated again seven coloured rays, and these were divided and redivided amongst the smaller stars [planets?] until they spread into the finest electric cobwebbing. Such a glorious vision it was, impossible fully to describe."

Moving their point of observation even higher, the author describes how she could see the etheric web going through and down, with the solar system appearing as a singular globe, and further still, "the solar systems were ... so small to our view that they looked like glowing planets. They were all swinging round in the orbit of the enormous golden star, which was evidently their sun."[31]

Benjamin Creme describes the same concept as follows: "The Plan of evolution is in the mind of that unbelievably high, evolved Cosmic Being Who ensouls planet Earth, our Planetary Logos. Our planet – with everything on it, including ourselves and all the creatures that ever walked the Earth – is the means of expression of that great Being. He has a plan for the evolution of this planet in relation to the greater Plan of the Solar Logos. The Solar Logos is an even more advanced Cosmic Being, Whose body of expression is the solar system, including this and all the other planets. All planets have a Planetary Logos Whose plans relate to that of the Solar Logos. He has an even greater Plan because He sees a wider meaning and purpose beyond what the Planetary Logoi are seeing and working towards."[32]

This hierarchical interrelatedness toward expressing a Consciousness that we as humans can know nothing about, let alone understand, shows how it would not make much sense that we would be visited by beings from outside our own system for the purpose of helping us grow in understanding. As a well-known principle says, "Natura non facit saltum" ('Nature doesn't jump'), in other words, we must learn to walk before we can run – whether physically, technologically or spiritually. And with several planets in our own system thousands, if not millions of years ahead of us in evolution, the Space Brothers from these planets have more to teach us along the lines of the plan of the solar Logos than we could assimilate even in the age of Aquarius that we are now entering.

In view of the above it looks far less, if at all, far-fetched when Benjamin Creme corroborates Adamski's contention that his contacts came from planets in our own solar system: "In my experience, what we call UFOs, the flying saucers, come from the planets of our own system. Not from the Pleiades, or Sirius or somewhere outside our own system, but from, mainly, Mars and Venus, although a few other planets like Jupiter and Mercury are also involved."[33]

Canadian UFO researcher Wilbert Smith seemed to hold the same view, although less publicly. In an article titled 'In

Defence of Wilbert Smith', Ronald Caswell wrote: "Smith had the habit of calling his extraterrestrial 'helpers' the Boys Topside. He referred to them as 'the people from elsewhere' or 'our friends from elsewhere'. (…) And whereas Adamski, for example, denoted the planets from whence his contacts came, i.e. Venus, Saturn, Mars, etc, – I believe that it was only in private that Wilbert Smith conjectured in this way." In the same article Mr Caswell documents that Smith's information could not have been based on George Adamski's account as the former had no extensive knowledge of the latter.[34] Bruno Ghibaudi also indicated, when asked, that the saucers "were coming from a number of places, including, perhaps, Mars and Venus."[35]

About contactees whom his Master has confirmed as genuine, but who insist that their contacts are from outside our solar system, Benjamin Creme has said: "Because it has been posited that life is impossible on the other planets of our system, some people, even with fairly authentic contact with the Space Brothers, insist that they come from outside our solar system – usually from the Pleiades. I personally do not believe this to be so. There is no overt contact between our civilization and that of the Pleiades."[36] Since everything in Cosmos is interconnected and interdependent, there are doubtless energetic connections at the level of the Solar Logos, but clearly these transcend contact with our planetary civilization. An educated guess as to the motives of contactees who claim otherwise would be that they are all too well aware of what happened to Adamski, as one of the very few who never wavered from the facts.

Echoing Adamski's refusal to authenticate the experiences of others, in the introduction to the Questions and Answers section in every issue of *Share International* magazine, as the editor Benjamin Creme asks his readers to refrain from asking questions about the validity of the work of others, saying he does "not seek to set himself up as the arbiter of the authenticity of other groups' activities and communications".

However, it seems he feels the topic of the origin of the space people to be of sufficient weight that, remarkably, he has deviated from his long-held policy in the case not only of Travis Walton (see Chapter 5), but also of Billy Meier, of whom Mr Creme has said: "I fully endorse the reality of the contacts but am convinced (and informed) that they are with people of our own Solar system."[37]

So, what we can fruitfully learn, we can only learn from the people who inhabit planets that are more advanced than our own *in our own solar system*. The only way more exalted Beings from higher systems could interact meaningfully with humanity is by taking incarnation in a human form, as in the case of some of the great Avatars of the East. However, because they come in to teach humanity about the divine origin and the oneness of all life, they would never draw attention to aspects of themselves that could create a sense of separation, and they would therefore never divulge where they are from. Moreover, at their level of advancement we may assume that space (or location, or distance) is of no importance to them whatsoever.

Planetary changes

In his latest book, *The Gathering of the Forces of Light – UFOs and their Spiritual Mission*, Benjamin Creme explains that the path of evolution for a planet is similar to that of our own evolution: "Instead of the thousands of incarnations that the soul has in the human evolution, the planets have seven major cycles, millions of years long. (...) Venus is in its last round, the seventh. (...) Both Mars and Earth are in the middle of the fourth round, at which time the planet 'awakens'. Enough has gone on before for the awakening of the true spiritual nature of the planet to become evident to the people, and more and more people are perfected. In that amazingly pregnant point in the middle of the fourth round everything starts afresh."[38] This would explain the events that are now unfolding on our planet, with millions of people rising up against oppression and injustice.

Such a planetary initiation is normally accompanied by great physical upheavals as well, as the magnetic poles of a planet usually shift at such times when there is a great planetary expansion of consciousness. And while, over the years, this notion has led many to announce wholesale destruction for everyone but a small group of their own followers, when asked if the "tilt of the Earth" would mean total destruction, George Adamski explained that "only a small portion of the planet will be directly affected". He added that this tilt is "a natural, orderly change which occurs to all planetary bodies" as a result of Nature "adhering to definite time cycles which cannot be altered by Man. (...) From above, where their vantage point gives a greater overall observation, and with their technical knowledge and more advanced instruments than any on Earth, the Brothers are watching... When findings are definite they will gladly share them with us. How much this could mean to us depends on how receptive we are when the time comes."[39] Elsewhere he added: "Many disturbances are now occurring in the world and will continue for several more years. This is because the world and even the system itself is in a great transition period."[40]

Many years later Benjamin Creme announced that "the 'Space Brothers', (...) mainly from Mars and Venus, but also from Jupiter, Mercury and a few other planets, have put around our planet a ring of light which keeps it on its axis. It is very slightly off its axis, but this ring allows it, within karmic limits, to be held so that the poles do not flip, which is predicted by so many 'prophets of doom' to take place. It will not take place. Nothing can shift that ring of light... Without their help this planet would probably be in chaos."[41] He later added that this ring of light was placed around the planet in 1979.[42]

Indeed, in his very first book, Benjamin Creme already gave the ultimate reason for the coming of the UFOs as "...basically a spiritual mission. Part of that mission is to hold this planet intact until the Forces of Light reach an energetic balance. This has been achieved. There was a period between 1956, roughly, and late 1959, when this world stood at the crossroads. The future of the world was really in the balance, and all efforts by Hierarchy and by the Hierarchy of some of the higher planets, especially Mars and Venus, were used to offset the mounting evil which was, in a sense, exploding on the planet – the last effort of the forces of evil to prevent the inauguration of the spiritual age of Aquarius; to prevent the externalisation of the Hierarchy and the Reappearance of the Christ*."[43]

An interesting concurrence can be found in Bruno Sammaciccia's account, who says: "Their mission over our Earth was to look after this planet, and above all after our safety, without interfering. And they told me that, since 1956, on at least two occasions they have had to prevent an atomic war..."[44]

Enrique Barrios has this explained by his protagonist Ami

---

* The term 'Christ' is used here to denote the office of the World Teacher within the Spiritual Hierarchy of Masters, Who is expected in all the major religions under different names: as the Christ by Christians; the Messiah by Jews; the fifth Buddha or Maitreya Buddha by Buddhists; the 10th incarnation of Vishnu or Kalki Avatar by Hindus; and the 12th Mahdi or Imam Mahdi by Muslims. These are the various religious expressions of the universal Doctrine of the Coming One, as it is known in the Ageless Wisdom teaching. See for instance Alice A. Bailey (1948), *The Reappearance of the Christ*, p.5 ff.

as follows: "You are approaching a decisive point in Earth evolution, a time when you either unite and bring about what some call the 'Age of Aquarius', or you destroy yourselves." The Age of Aquarius, according to Ami, is "a new evolutionary stage of the planet Earth, the end of millennia of barbarism, a New Age of love, a kind of 'mutation'. You have already entered the 'Age of Aquarius', but only in time, not in deed. The Earth begins to be ruled by other kinds of laws and cosmic geological radiations. To put it another way, there is more love in people, but they still continue to follow principles that belonged to earlier, inferior levels of evolution. What occurs is a clash between what people feel internally, and what they are obliged to do externally."[45] Such is the magnitude of the occasion, of this time of transition, although few, if any, of even the best informed UFO researchers seem to be aware of its connection to their subject.

The social upheavals that we are now witnessing around the globe in the form of mass popular protests in demand of freedom and justice are also a result of this initiatory process and were indeed foretold by Adamski in his 1962 article 'World Disturbances': "Not only geophysical disturbances will occur, but many will occur in society itself. Those occurring in society will be of many shades and variations. The certainty that man hopes for, peace of mind and of the world, will not come until the transition period is over. (...) The old must go before the new can be born to fulfill its services to mankind. The wise will observe each act of the change, the fool may run amuck and destroy himself."[46]

In all this, therefore, humanity also has its responsibility when it comes to the causes of some of the problems on our planet, as well as their solutions. Since we have a definite part to play in the spiritualization of matter, which is the nearest we can come to a definition of the Plan of Evolution in the mind of our planetary Logos, we are not only accountable for the destruction of the natural world which forms our habitat, but also for the divisions and the wars, and the suffering as a result of which we are inflicting on our fellow human beings. This we are told not only by our Elder Brothers, the Masters of Wisdom, but by the Brothers from space as well.

Although the extraterrestrials could destroy our nuclear weapons, according to Italian journalist Bruno Ghibaudi, "the human heart would nevertheless remain unchanged", which is why he says they work in subtler ways to influence the human mind: "They fully realize the dangers of any kind of broad prohibitive action. They know that in the last analysis Earth-Man must make his own way..."[47]

A poignant example of these "subtler ways" in which the space people are helping Earth humanity was described by Wilbert Smith in a speech given in Ottawa on 31 March 1958, as follows: "The people from 'elsewhere' displayed great patience and understanding in helping me to overcome many of the prejudices and stories of misinformation which I had spent many years accumulating. I began for the first time to realise the basic 'ONENESS' of the Universe and all that is in it. (...) One of the most important things I had to realise is that we are not alone. The human race in the form of MAN extends throughout the Universe, and is incredibly ancient..." He goes on to say: "The question might be asked – 'If these people really are our brothers and are interested in our welfare, why do they remain so aloof?' We have been given the answer. There is a basic law of the Universe which grants each and every individual independence and freedom of choice, so that he may experience and learn from his experiences. No-one has the right to interfere in the affairs of others – in fact, our Ten Commandments are directives against interference. If we disregard this law we must suffer the consequences, and a little thought will show that the present deplorable world state is directly attributable to violation of this principle."[48]

Asked why the extraterrestrials won't stop the wars, Michael Wolf, in his book *The Catchers of Heaven*, gives an identical reason: "A kind of 'non-intervention directive' like in Star Trek, that humans would resent any enforced peace. Yes, many powers on this earth would resent such an act, even if it were something they desired, and the fact that they haven't done it for themselves, that it was forced upon them."[49]

In *Angels in Starships,* that was first published in Italian in 1983, Giorgio Dibitonto describes how he and two of his friends are contacted by the Space Brothers in 1980 and, over a period of many months, are trained for more intensive contacts and experiences. Eventually they are taken on several journeys in spacecraft, where exalted beings teach them valuable lessons about life on Earth and on other planets. Mr Dibitonto and his companions are also asked to extend warnings of impending catastrophe if humanity does not change its course.

Remarkably, in his foreword the publisher, the late Wendelle Stevens, relates his interview with Benjamin Creme who confirmed that the author was introduced to the very same space people whom Adamski had introduced to the world in his books as the Saturnians Ramu (who introduced himself to Dibitonto as Raphael) and Zuhl, the Venusians Orthon and Kalna, the Martians Firkon and Ilmuth, as well as a space person who lived on earth as... George Adamski.

In a clear reference to the importance of understanding the oneness of life, Dibitonto and his companions are told by Orthon: "The under-developed state of many parts of the world results in starvation and death through undernourishment and disease, as a consequence of poverty. That is a very heavy burden of guilt to be borne by those people who have a thriving culture."[50] Earlier Raphael had hinted at the wider consequences of the state of our planet by saying: "The Earth is out of harmony, and disintegrating vibrations, like the scourges that lash her sorrowing multitudes, create ever-widening zones on the planet where the life energies are undermined. One day you will understand the reality of these conditions which are beyond the grasp of your limited science. Those few who have begun to realize the true situation are misunderstood and left alone."[51]

Conscious connections

On one of his visits to a mothership Giorgio Dibitonto describes how his hosts were keen for him and his companions to understand the energetic and spiritual foundation of our life in the three worlds (of physical, emotional and mental expression) and he describes how they were shown the etheric counterparts of our solid physical bodies: "The clothing of the three persons seemed to dissolve in a meld of pastel shades, then rearrange themselves until we could see three well-dressed persons, a man, a woman and child who were the same, and yet not the same as before. The flesh tones seemed now to have a shimmering light blue quality, as if lit up by some inner radiant source. The bodies seemed somehow lighter than the previous ones. It was as if two bodies were superimposed, one over the other. We could clearly discern the separate bodies of each of the three persons, yet they appeared as one."

"In this way," explained Ilmuth, "you can visually comprehend the various dimensions of the life-force in man, in the world of plants, and in the mineral kingdom."[52] Indeed, it goes a long way to illustrate the interconnectedness of all life which the space visitors seem to think is important since, according to Adamski, "we are being alerted to the existence of neighbors in space by their craft through our atmosphere. Prior to proof of their reality, a large majority of the people were unaware of human inhabitants on other planets. It is their sincere hope to bring us into the family of our Solar System through knowledge."[53]

Despite the unmistakable Christian overtones in the author's narration, in a subtle, indefinable way Mr Dibitonto's description breaks down the barrier between our conscious experience of dense physical life on Earth and, not just life on other planets, but, it seems, life on the higher, inner planes of existence, as a result leaving the reader with a vivid experience of our place in cosmos as the body of the Creator, where humanity will only be allowed to roam free when it realizes, and *acts from an experience of*, its essential oneness with all.

Further testimony to this much expanded view of life comes from Mexican contactee Carlos Díaz, whose contacts with extraterrestrials started in January 1981 when he saw and photographed a large, oval-shaped orange UFO at about 30 metres from his car while on an assignment for a magazine at Ajusco Park near Mexico City. It was not until March that year that he was first contacted by what he describes as human-looking extraterrestrials, which he says continues to this day.[54] Mr Díaz says that through his contacts he has been imbued with an awareness of the interconnectedness of all life and the need to preserve the environment, strongly reminiscent of the messages given to other contactees. His experiences taught Díaz that every living entity on Earth is important for the whole: "I have experienced that there is a wonderful interaction between all living things. But this interaction has been disturbed. Every individual, every species is an important part of this interaction."

A similar notion, again, is conveyed to Enrique Barrios, whose alter ego 'Pete' wonders how some people could still be in denial about the existence of people elsewhere in cosmos. Ami answers: "Those people are naïve; not only do we exist, we also watch carefully. If you use espionage as a means of defense, it would be foolish to think that we don't observe you." In confirmation of Vera Stanley Alder's experience (pages 136-38), he continues: "The whole universe is a single unity, a living organism ... we can't overlook scientific discoveries produced on any uncivilized world. I told you that certain powers in evil hands could alter the whole equilibrium of the galaxy ... and that includes our worlds, everything affects everything else..." Ami also told Pete: "[I]f your people don't change now, if you continue to deplete your planet's resources – polluting the air, water and food as if there were no tomorrow – there will be no tomorrow!"[55]

Through his experiences, Carlos Díaz says, he has come to realize that we are going through a crucial stage in human history in which our carelessness is destroying nature and the vitality of the planet. But, he says, our creativity can bring about transformation: "We have to realize that the future of us and our planet is in our hands. (...) My intention in sharing this is to invite people to act. I want to invite people to listen to the existence of extraterrestrial life, and this experience has made me aware of the wonderful home that we have. And I do believe that if we learn to respect and love life the encounter with them will be inevitable."[56]

It could probably not have been put more clearly than Amicizia participant Paolo di Girolamo did, when he said: "The most fascinating part of [the space people's] affirmations on the relation between mankind and the universe is that of the reality, already imagined by the philosophers of the past, of an existential integration between microcosm and the macrocosm."[57]

Having broadened our view of life to the point where we see that it is all there is – indeed the *cause* of all there is – and that it would not be logical for space travellers from higher systems to visit us when we have so much to learn from our more evolved brothers and sisters within our own solar system, it is not difficult to understand that the evolution of form only facilitates the evolution of consciousness. As Adamski said: "[T]hat which we call spirit could not manifest if it were not for [a] material form through which to express; nor could the material exist if it were not for the spirit, or Cause."[58] However, both need to proceed in step. And while it is clear that our technological advancement has outpaced our moral and ethical progress, there are those who see a breakthrough in consciousness on the horizon.

One of these is Ervin László, a Hungarian philosopher of science, systems theorist and integral theorist, who has developed a theory of the universe as a living creature. He founded the Club of Budapest in the likeness of the Club of Rome (which was established in 1968 and gained worldwide recognition for its 1972 report 'The Limits to Growth'), to "center attention on the evolution of human values and consciousness as the crucial factors in changing course – from a race toward degradation, polarization, and disaster to a rethinking of values and priorities so as to navigate today's transformation in the direction of humanism, ethics, and global sustainability". The Club of Budapest has had among its members high-standing clergymen, scientists, and artists such as the Dalai Lama, Mikhail Gorbachev, Liv Ullmann, Elie Wiesel, Vaclav Havel, and the late Yehudi Menuhin and Peter Ustinov.

In an interview in 2008 László revealed that he has had access to information about contacts with extraterrestrials, although he added that it was meant to be kept very confidential. But despite the fact that he declined to divulge many details ("because they will never tell me anything anymore"), he said: "I am certain that contact has been made."[59]

A veritable Renaissance man, in addition to being a scientist and a philosopher Dr László is also a classical pianist who has recorded several works. László says that it is no coincidence that many scientists are also good musicians, because "music especially, but all forms of art, give you this sense of oneness, a sense of wholeness. Now, all great scientists and all great artists are looking for a sense of oneness".

László says that we are at a tipping point in the history of our planet, which he calls the 'chaos point'. He explains it as "the point where we either break down, or go forward in a different and a new way. We are approaching that point," László said in an interview on Dutch television at the end of 2006.[60] "We have to live on this planet in a way that everyone could share its resources. Right now we are overusing these capacities. If we don't act, then the breakdown will come. And I don't think we will act if we don't understand. You have to say, 'This is my priority. I want to achieve a sustainable world, for myself, for my children, for all people. It starts with understanding, but it carries forward with value change, and basically the evolution of our consciousness."

According to László, one of the basic elements of spirituality that has also been incorporated in religions is the concept of Oneness: "We are not separate. One of the key problems that we have is the sense that 'I am separate'. 'It doesn't concern me what happens to you, what happens to Nature, what happens to other people, because they are not me.' Dividing the world into 'me' and 'not me' – that is at the root of our problems and that's why we need spirituality and religion."

"I believe that people are awakening. People recognize that if we don't change, we're going to run into serious problems – climate problems, poverty problems, food problems, cultural conflicts, war. I believe gradually, and perhaps even more rapidly now, there is a change in people's mind sets, and that is what counts. Ultimately, change yourself, change your consciousness, and then try to act differently."

"Thinking and acting go together. If you just think and go and meditate in a corner then that is not much help. You have to also act. It has to do with lifestyles, it has to do with consumer behaviour, the products we buy, how we furnish our house, how we communicate with others, what kind of political behaviour we have, what kind of leaders we choose, what kind of companies we want to patronize. But key to everything that we do is the thought: 'Is what I do compatible for 6.5 to 7 billion people on this Earth? Or am I using so much energy, so many resources, producing so much waste, that if everyone would live like that the whole thing would just go to pieces?' In other words: 'Do I live in a sustainable way?' That is the new ethics, the new philosophy. Ask yourself: Is what I do sustainable?"

László says that we have everything we need to take on the challenge; we only lack the will, because we don't have the vision yet: "We haven't yet woken up to the seriousness and the urgency of the problem. This is why I say, wake up! We have five or six years. We have to do it. We can do it."

His assurance was echoed recently in an article by economist David Korten, who said: "As I witness the devastation wrought by the Old Economy, my greatest source of sadness comes from an awareness of the profound gap between our human reality and our human possibility." Yet, he says, "We are privileged to live at the most exciting moment of creative opportunity in the whole of the human experience. Now is the hour. We have the power to turn this world around for the sake of ourselves and our children for generations to come. We are the ones we have been waiting for."[61]

A declaration of hope

As we can see the existing structures failing and crumbling before our eyes, with countries becoming ever more difficult to govern and indeed governments ever more difficult to form, with leaders who lack the vision or the skills to tackle the challenges of broken economic and financial systems, societies and communities falling apart for the failures of our social and educational systems, it might be easy to lose sight of professor László's optimistic views and fall prey to despair, as is no doubt the experience of many who lack the broader view of reality which this chapter describes.

At the same time, more and more people show their willingness to stand up and be counted, sending a strong message to their governments that the affairs of humanity can no longer be conducted on a 'business as usual' basis while everyone can see that the old ways and 'solutions' are not working anymore. Just as the people in the Middle East, who have overcome their decades of trepidation in the face of unforgiving absolute rulers, and now increasingly the people in so-called Western democracies where corporate powers have consumed any semblance of democracy, over the past decade or so a movement has also swelled up from the ranks of UFO truth seekers whose tenacity is increasingly embarrassing governments that entrusted the facts of the extraterrestrial presence to undemocratic, secretive bodies, while the space people themselves seem to be ever more ready to up the pressure on governments from their end as they show more and more of themselves in increasingly spectacular sightings around the world.

At the same time it is clear that, if governments would make statements about the knowledge they have been keeping from the public, they would be, in the words of Benjamin Creme, "committing political suicide".[62] However, distinct indications are offered from various corners that this is a time like none other. As Giorgio Dibitonto was told by the Martian Firkon, for instance, signaling support for humanity in its present travail: "No single event that ever yet happened on Earth, can compare with that which stands before you now. ... Clouds and pillars of fire, which today you would call flying saucers and motherships, were seen over the leaders of the Hebrews who fled from Egypt. Exactly the same signs and realities portend in these days a new and final journey, which will lead you out of your present misery, into the true promised land of universal love. It is most important that all people understand this. The time is short."

Ilmuth added reassuringly: "We will accompany you, as we did in those days, and our presence will be much more in evidence this time. ... [Humanity] will travel through a wilderness, in comparison to which the one that the Hebrews overcame would seem like an oasis. But we will be over you as before, only more visibly, to aid and comfort you." The Venusian Kalna elaborated: "The Hebrews were led by a great universal brother, who was born here in order to fulfill this important mission. His name was Moses. You will be led by a new Moses whom we all love and admire greatly. He will lead all the people on this new exodus, like a good brother or father. ... The message that we bring you from the universe is one of hope and salvation, during this time when dark clouds are gathering on the horizons of planet Earth."[63]

What should be clear by now is that these "dark clouds" are mostly of our own making, having thus far failed to see the oneness of the human family as the solution to the problems which we have insisted on tackling from our age-old sense of separation. That separation has created the conditions for our very own 'wilderness experience', where the old certainties seem to be dropping by the wayside one by one, as the political, economic, financial, social, and environmental crises are coming together in a 'perfect storm'.

If the problems are the result of ignorance or, in some cases, of ignoring our innate oneness, the sense of separation from our brothers and sisters which causes us to fear that we might lose out in the struggle for survival – despite the fact that we inhabit a bountiful planet and actually produce a food surplus of 10 per cent per capita, even with the current overpopulation – and which has informed our present systems that are based on competition, then the solution must be in its opposite.

It is again Enrique Barrios who expresses the underlying truths in the easiest to understand terms in his book, *Ami, Child of the Stars*. When Pete is finally ready to learn that love is the "Fundamental Law of the Universe" Ami tells him: "It's simple and natural, however it isn't too easy to experience, that's what evolution is for. Evolution means to approach love. The most evolved beings express and experience more love. The less evolved beings express and experience less love." He further explains to his Earth friend that we have a barrier inside us that prevents this expression: "The bigger the ego, the more important we consider ourselves to be in relation to the rest. The ego makes us feel authorized to devalue, harm, dominate and use others; even to direct their lives. Since ego is a barrier to love, it keeps us from feeling compassion, tenderness, affection... love. The ego desensitizes us against life."[64]

The same obstacle was addressed by Albert Einstein in a letter of 1950: "A human being is a part of a whole, called by us universe, a part limited in time and space. He experiences himself, his thoughts and feelings as something separated from the rest... a kind of optical delusion of his consciousness. This delusion is a kind of prison for us, restricting us to our personal desires and to affection for a few persons nearest to us. Our task must be to free ourselves from this prison by widening our circle of compassion to embrace all living creatures and the whole of nature in its beauty."[65] Likewise, the Teachers of mankind have been informing us, throughout the ages, but especially in the information coming from Benjamin Creme and pertinent to the state of the world now, that we will only survive on this planet if we realize that we are One, and begin to give expression to that realization by creating economic and social justice for everyone.

To his statement quoted above, Einstein added that nobody can achieve that freedom completely, "but the striving for such achievement is in itself a part of the liberation and a foundation for inner security." Or, as Ami explained to his young terrestrial friend Pete: "We should try to be ourselves [i.e. express the love that we are made of], that is freedom... There is no other freedom..."[66]

So how could we expect enough members of the human race to be convinced that a civilization based on sharing and co-operation is even a viable goal? Surely people will not be able or willing to give up their conditioning of thousands of years? According to some, though, we are in for a momentous watershed and, they say, that is why the Space Brothers are here in this difficult time of transition.

Even in 1963 Alberto Perego wrote: "They [the space people] foresee a future of great prosperity for planet Earth, if our leaders will avoid a new conflict and will confirm that they are among us, to help us. Based on the events of the last twenty years, we have no reasons to doubt this. We must not forget, indeed, that we owe it to them that thus far no nuclear war has broken out.

"Also, according to the extraterrestrial pilots, given the technological means that we already possess (press, radio, television, air force) it would only take a few months for our political and religious leaders to inform the whole planet of the new reality. In this way we could inaugurate a new era."[67]

In his 1958 novel *The Amazing Mr Lutterworth* Desmond Leslie gives a fictitious account of one way this might happen. The story ends in a dramatic scene in which the Space Brother who is the protagonist inaugurates the "Time of Splendour" by distributing the key to unlimited free and clean energy to all the countries of the world, so that it cannot be cornered by any person, corporation or nation on Earth. This the Brother does as he mentally overshadows all the members of the General Assembly of the United Nations organization, while he conveys this message: "This power (...) shall change the face of the Earth. No more shall small groups, nor even single men, be able to rule multitudes through hunger in their bellies; for there shall no more be hunger nor want nor cold; and in time again there shall be no more disease, for as man learns to live in harmony with nature, instead of continually struggling against it, he will destroy the cause of disease."[68]

It should be remembered that, although published as a novel, the author later said that the story was 75 per cent non-fiction, as it was based on the mission of George Adamski.[69] Also, Leslie's fictitious reference to a new civilization is echoed in an article which Wilbert Smith wrote around the same time, in the late 1950s. In 'The Philosophy of the Saucers' Smith says: "In time, when certain events have transpired, and we are so oriented that we can accept these people from elsewhere, they will meet us freely on common ground of mutual understanding and trust. We will be able to learn from them and bring about the Golden Age all men everywhere desire deep within their hearts."[70]

This new civilization will come about when we begin to build the structures that allow us to express more of our spiritual nature. As Ami tells Pete: "The problem is not in the people, but in the systems they use. People have evolved, but systems have remained backward. Bad systems make good people suffer. These systems make people unhappy, which finally turns them bad. A good system of global organization can easily turn bad into good."[71]

The hands-on experience of the oneness of life which esotericist and author Vera Stanley Alder describes in her autobiography *From the Mundane to the Magnificent*, concludes with a vision of the future of the planet which she was granted. Witnessing a world that she describes as "very desirable and ideal", she cannot help but wonder "what could possibly happen to change the world so much?" Her teacher answers: "Mankind has determined, with his famous free-will, to learn his lessons the hard way, through the stimulation of almost outrageous suffering and degradation. But evolution *must* go on, and its stimulation will eventually stir up humanity so that all the dregs and repressions will rise to the surface. Thus people will be shown their present state so clearly that a worldwide reaction, revulsion and aspiration will take place."

In what seems an almost literal reference to what Giorgio Dibitonto was told by his contacts from space, Mrs Alder's teacher continues: "This change will enable the greatest event in world history to take place. (...) Christ told us that He would come again. The Jews believe in the coming of the Messiah; in the East they await Matreya [sic]. The ancient Egyptians ... spoke of the Ever-Coming One, who appeared in each Sign of the Zodiac, to give humanity its next lesson in evolution."

The book in which Mrs Alder describes the vision that she was given in 1942 was first published in 1979, which means she was writing it before Benjamin Creme's first book had been published. Yet, her description of this event which will shake humanity out of its fear and complacency, is almost identical with how Creme has been presenting it: "People were streaming silently into [a large and beautiful college] from all directions... A golden light gradually built up on the screen. It blazed with ever greater intensity until a figure suddenly appeared in its midst. I could hardly bear to look at Him. But He soon began to speak. His words were very few and very slow. They seemed to instil meaning and realization other than physically. I felt a great communication at work in the hall."[72]

According to Mr Creme, this world event will in fact be witnessed by everyone around the world when, on the Day of Declaration, the World Teacher, whose personal name is Maitreya, will be invited to address humanity in a worldwide television broadcast, as a result of the rising pressure on governments that is now building around the world. While we will see His face on our TV screens, we will hear His words inwardly, each in their own language, as He mentally overshadows everyone over 14 years of age. As His energy of Love, of which He is the embodiment on this planet, flows out in enormous strength, everyone will experience the spiritual essence of their being and the innate oneness of humanity.

Benjamin Creme has always been happy to leave it to the events that are unfolding in our time to prove the accuracy of his statements, which he has presented throughout as mere information, never as dogma. To a question whether he is infallible and, if not, how we could know when he was right or wrong, Mr Creme replied: "I am not infallible; not even the

Masters claim infallibility. So yes, I agree, you have a problem. Only the intuition, and the discriminating faculty that comes with long years of direct experience in association with a Master, allows one to *publicly* make the statements I do."[73]

However, with corroborations coming independently from an English portraitist's experience in 1942, Desmond Leslie's fictionalized story of George Adamski's mission, and more directly from the space contacts of Wilbert Smith, consul Perego and Giorgio Dibitonto, there is good reason to learn what Mr Creme has to say about the disclosure of the information that governments and the military have of the extraterrestrial presence on our planet: "The governments will only act when they are forced to do it. When Maitreya [the World Teacher] is known openly, He will be asked questions (...), and the truth of the relationship between this planet and the other planets will become known. Then the people from other planets will land [openly] and the reality of their existence will be known. ... [T]he knowledge, the acceptance of the reality of the Space Brothers, will come through the acceptance of Maitreya and the Masters of our Spiritual Hierarchy. They will confirm that the Space Brothers are real, that the spaceships are real, that the other planets have their citizens who have nothing but goodwill, who are harmless, who want to help each other, and who will help this planet in so far as the law of karma allows."[74]

If this notion is correct, what we are seeing in the news and witnessing in the streets at this time is nothing less than mankind indicating its readiness for the inauguration of Perego's "new era", Leslie's "Time of Splendour", Smith's "Golden Age", or, as Enrique Barrios, Vera Stanley Alder and Benjamin Creme call it, the new age of Aquarius – the age of justice and freedom for all – by Maitreya, the World Teacher, and the Masters of Wisdom, with the help of our Brothers and Sisters from space.

Notes

1 George Adamski (1955), *Inside the Space Ships*, p.180
2 Lou Zinsstag & Timothy Good (1983), *George Adamski – The Untold Story*, p.88
3 Adamski (1965), *Cosmic Bulletin*, p.2
4 Adamski (1965a), *Answers to Questions Most Frequently Asked About Our Space Visitors and Other Planets*, p.12
5 Stefano Breccia (2009), *Mass Contacts*, p.188
6 Ivan Ceci (2011a), 'Witness of Italian extraterrestrial contact case emerges'. ExoNews, [online] 15 August. Available at <news.exopoliticsinstitute.org/ index.php/interview-with-italian-witness-of-et-contact91/> [Accessed 3 September 2011]
7 Breccia (2009), op cit, pp.240-41
8 Michael Wolf (1993), *The Catchers of Heaven*, 1996 reprint, p.201
9 Adamski (1955), op cit, pp.88-89
10 Adamski (1957-58), *Cosmic Science for the promotion of Cosmic Principles and Truths*, Series 1, Part 2, Question #39
11 Enrique Barrios (1989), *Ami, Child of the Stars*, p.21
12 Benjamin Creme (2010), *The Gathering of the Forces of Light – UFOs and their Spiritual Mission*, p.46
13 Creme (2001), *The Great Approach – New Light and Life for Humanity*, p.135

Law and order

14 Creme (2001), op cit, p.129
15 Ibidem, p.131
16 Creme (2010), op cit, p.86
17 Adamski (1957-58), op cit, Part 1, Question #5
18 Breccia (2009), op cit, p.244
19 Barrios (1989), op cit, pp.19-20
20 Adamski, *Wisdom of the Masters of the Far East* (1936), 2000 reprint, p.24
21 Creme (2011), 'Questions and Answers', *Share International* magazine Vol.30, No.6, July/August, p.35
22 Creme (2010a), 'Questions and Answers', *Share International* magazine Vol.29, No.6, July/August, p.35
23 Creme (1979), *The Reappearance of the Christ and the Masters of Wisdom*, p.209
24 Alice A. Bailey, *Discipleship in the New Age*, Vols 1 (1944) and 2 (1955)
25 Adamski (1957-58), op cit, Part 4, Question #72
26 Yogi Ramacharaka (1909), *Lessons in Gnani Yoga – The Yoga of Wisdom*. Yogi Ramacharaka was the name used to publish the books written by American New Thought writer William Walker Atkinson in co-operation

with Baba Bharata, a disciple of the real Yogi Ramacharaka, an Indian initiate who lived from 1799-1893.

27 Masaru Emoto (1999), *Messages from Water*
28 Creme (2002), 'Questions and answers'. *Share International* Vol.21, No.1, January/February, p.47
29 Alexander Lauterwasser (2007), *Water Sound Images: The Creative Music of the Universe*
30 Barrios (1989), op cit, p.65
31 Vera Stanley Alder (1979), *From the Mundane to the Magnificent – A Volume of Autobiography*, pp.42-49
32 Creme (2010), op cit, p.115
33 Ibid., p.61
34 Ronald Caswell (1967), 'In Defence of Wilbert Smith'. *UFO Contact* Vol 2., No.8, December, p.205
35 Gordon W. Creighton (1963), 'The Italian Scene – Part 3: Bruno Ghibaudi's contact claim'. *Flying Saucer Review* Vol.9, No.3, May-June, p.19
36 Creme (2010), op cit, p.47
37 Creme (2010a), 'Questions and answers', *Share International* Vol.29, No.10, December, p.27

Planetary changes
38 Creme (2010), op cit, p.45
39 Adamski (1957-58), op cit Part 2, Question No.32
40 Adamski (1962), 'World Disturbances'. *Cosmic Science* newsletter Vol.1, No.1, January 1962, p.4
41 Creme (2001), op cit, p.130
42 Creme (2010a), op cit
43 Creme (1979), op cit, p.211
44 Breccia (2009), op cit, p.239
45 Barrios (1989), op cit, pp.99-100
46 Adamski (1962), op cit
47 Timothy Good (1998), *Alien Base – Earth's Encounters with Extraterrestrials*, pp.216-17
48 Wilbert B. Smith (1958), speech given 31 March in Ottowa, Canada. Transcript published in *Flying Saucer Review* Vol.9, No.5, September-October 1963, pp.14-15
49 Wolf (1993), op cit, p.323
50 Giorgio Dibitonto (1990), *Angels in Starships*, p.82
51 Ibid., pp.20-21

Conscious connections
52 Dibitonto (1990) op cit, pp.71-72
53 Adamski (1957-58), op cit, Part 1, Question No.4

54 *The X Factor* (1989), 'Carlos Díaz'. Issue 89, p.2469
55 Barrios (1989), op cit. p.76
56 Interview with Carlos Díaz in Michael Hesemann (dir.; 2001), *Ships of Light – The Carlos Díaz Experience*. Available at <www.youtube.com/ watch?v=SaAluEBxXLI>
57 Paolo di Girolamo (2009), *Noi e Loro*, p.141
58 Adamski (1957-58), op cit, Part 2, Question No.38
59 Interview with Ervin László in Tessa Koops (2008), 'Tessa Koops meets...' Available at: <www.disclose.tv/action/viewvideo/4817/ Ervin_Laszlo__Contact _with_Extraterrestials_soon_2>
60 Interview with Ervin László in Annemiek Schrijver (2006), 'Het Alziend Oog'. IKON TV, 31 December. Available at <tvblik.nl/alziend-oog/ ervin-laszlo>
61 David Korten (2011), 'The Path to Real Prosperity'. *YES! Magazine* [online] 7 September. Available at <www.yesmagazine.org/blogs/ david-korten/the-path-to-real-prosperity> [Accessed 10 September 2011]

A declaration of hope
62 Creme (2010), op cit, p.37
63 Dibitonto (1990), op cit, pp.32-33
64 Barrios (1989), op cit., pp.79-80
65 As quoted in *The New York Times*, 29 March 1972. Source: <en.wikiquote.org/wiki/Albert_Einstein> [Accessed 28 August 2011]
66 Barrios (1989), op cit., p.105
67 Alberto Perego (1963), *L'aviazione di altri pianeti opera tra noi: rapporto agli italiani: 1943-1963*, p.536
68 Desmond Leslie (1958), *The Amazing Mr Lutterworth*, p.202
69 Zinsstag & Good (1983), op cit, p.78
70 Smith (n.d.), 'The Philosophy of the Saucers'. Available at <www.presidentialufo.com/wilbert-smith-articles/125-the-philosophy- of-the-saucers> [Accessed 28 March 2011]
71 Barrios (1989), op cit., pp.37-38
72 Alder (1979), op cit, pp.198-99
73 Creme (2010a), op cit
74 Creme (2010), op cit, pp.50-51

Epilogue

It should be understood that while there are many similarities to be found in the reports coming from contactees, past and present, as this book shows, they also diverge on several points.

As indicated in the second chapter, the selection of the similarities chosen for this book was not random, but based on their direct or tangential concurrence with the teachings of the ages. After all, contradictions or dichotomies in contactees' reports may be due to reasons ranging from limited perception; a lack of understanding; distortion in the information conveyed due to either of the former or life-long conditioning; the need for fictionalization; or fear of ridicule. Such discrepancies, however, are for these very reasons of far less importance than statements that not only mutually support each other, but confirm the tenets of the Ageless Wisdom as well. Additionally, very much misinformation has been fed to people who may or may not have had genuine contacts, with the sole purpose of obscuring the facts and confusing the public perception of the extra-terrestrial presence. It is hoped that with the reference framework provided here, readers will find themselves better equipped to separate the wheat from all that chaff.

Many of the conspiracy adherents say we have a duty to inform and educate ourselves; "knowledge protects" is one of their slogans and no-one in their right mind would deny the importance of knowledge. But if that 'knowledge' is based on speculation posing as 'research' and alleged 'facts' that result from ignorance and fear, it will only perpetuate ignorance and fear, and thereby prolong mankind's struggle towards the light of justice, freedom and peace for all.

Knowing that all life is interconnected and that humanity is essentially one, the state of the world leaves us in no doubt that the crises facing us are really spiritual in nature too: only when we begin to look after our fellow human beings, placing their well-being above economic, political or military interests, and sharing the bounty of the planet among all, will we be expressing our true nature as spiritual beings.

So effective was the conspiracy to deny the experiences and facts as reported by the early contactees, that critical thinking has now largely become conspiracy thinking. But instead of just that battle, we would let the forces of materiality win the disinformation war if we allowed breakaway imagination to distract us from the real challenges at hand, which are man-made and the result of our inability to see that humanity is one, and act on that fact.

As many people are now aware, "energy follows thought" or, in other words, we energize what we pay attention to and align ourselves with. So if we agree on the need to inform ourselves, we first need to decide what we want to inform ourselves of – speculation that increases fear, based on the ways of the past, or rather ignored or forgotten facts that inspire hope for the future of mankind based on the wisdom tradition of both terrestrial and extraterrestrial origin.

Only the latter will allow us to see where the responsibility for what happens next on our planet rests: in the hands of each of us individually, where it has always been.

APPENDIX

The Golden Rule
(The Law of Harmlessness)
as expressed in various religious traditions

Baha'i
"Lay not on any soul a load that you would not wish to be laid upon you, and desire not for anyone the things you would not desire for yourself." –*Baha'u'llah, Gleanings*

Buddhism
"Treat not others in ways that you yourself would find hurtful." –*Gautama Buddha, Udana-Varga 5:18*

Confucianism
"Do not do to others what you do not want done to yourself." –*Confucius, Analects 15.23*

Christianity
"Therefore all things whatsoever ye would that men should do to you, do ye even so to them: for this is the law and the prophets." –*Jesus, Matthew 7:12*

Hinduism
"One should never do that to another which one regards as injurious to one's own self. This, in brief, is the rule of Righteousness." –*Mahabharata, Anusasana Parva 113.8*

Islam
"Not one of you truly believes until you wish for your brothers what you wish for yourself." –*the Prophet Muhammad, Forty Hadith of an-Nawawi 13*

Jainism
"One should treat all creatures in the world as one would like to be treated." –*Mahavira, Sutrakritanga 1.11.33*

Judaism
"What is hateful to you, do not do to your neighbor. This is the whole Law; all the rest is commentary." –*Hillel, Talmud, Shabbat 31a*

Native American
"Do not wrong or hate your neighbor. For it is not he who you wrong, but yourself." –*Pima proverb*

Sikhism
"I am a stranger to no one; and no one is a stranger to me. Indeed, I am a friend to all." –*Guru Granth Sahib, p.1299*

Taoism
"Regard your neighbour's gain as your own gain, and your neighbour's loss as your own loss." –*T'ai Shang Kan Ying P'ien, 213-218*

Wicca
"An ye harm none, do what ye will." –*Wiccan Rede*

Zoroastrianism
"Whatever is disagreeable to yourself, do not do unto others." –*Shayast-na-Shayast 13:29*

Sources and references

India Daily. 'China and India both know about underground UFO base in the Himalayan border area deep into the tectonic plates', 9 January 2005

New York Times. 'Air Force Order on "Saucers" Cited – Pamphlet by the Inspector General Called Objects a "Serious Business"'. 28 February 1960.

The X Factor. 'Carlos Díaz', Issue 89, 2000 (UK, London: Marshall Cavendish Ltd)

'Cutler-Twining Memo', 14 July 1954

'Former Legislator Makes Statement on Un-Released Eisenhower Brief', 8 May 2010

'Majestic Twelve Project – Annual Report', n.d. (1952?)

Gerard Aartsen. 'The Friendship Case: Space Brothers teach lessons of brotherhood'. *Share International* magazine Vol.30, No.3, April 2011

Gerard Aartsen. *George Adamski – A Herald for the Space Brothers* (the Netherlands, Amsterdam: BGA Publications, 2010)

Gerard Aartsen. *Our Elder Brothers Return – A History in Books* (the Netherlands, Amsterdam: BGA Publications, 2008); published online at www.biblioteca-ga.info

Benjamin Adamah. "De Illuminati bestaan niet". Lecture for Delft University of Technology Studium Generale, 3 November 2008

George Adamski. *Answers to Questions Most Frequently Asked About Our Space Visitors and Other Planets* (USA, Palomar Gardens, CA: G. Adamski, 1965)

George Adamski. *Cosmic Science for the promotion of Cosmic Principles and Truths*. (USA, Valley Center, CA: Cosmic Science, 1957-58)

George Adamski. *Flying Saucers Farewell*. (USA, New York, NY: Abelard-Schuman, 1961)

George Adamski. *Inside the Space Ships* (USA, New York, NY: Abelard-Schumann, 1955)

George Adamski. *Many Mansions* (USA, Detroit, MI: Interplanetary Relations, 1955), 1974 reprint

George Adamski. *Pioneers of Space* (USA, Los Angeles, CA: Leonard-Freefield, 1949)

George Adamski. 'The Space People' (1964). In: Gerard Aartsen, *George Adamski – A Herald for the Space Brothers*, 2010

George Adamski. *Wisdom of the Masters of the Far East* (USA, Laguna Beach, CA: Royal Order of Tibet, 1936), Health Research reprint, 2000

Vera Stanley Alder. *From the Mundane to the Magnificent – A Volume of Autobiography*. (UK, London: Rider Books, 1979)

Orfeo Angelucci. *The Secret of the Saucers.* (USA, Amherst, WI: The Amherst Press, 1955)

Alice A. Bailey. *Discipleship in the New Age*, Vols 1 (UK, London: Lucis Trust, 1944, 11th printing, 1985) and 2 (1955, 6th printing, 1980)

Alice A. Bailey. *The Externalization of the Hierarchy* (UK, London: Lucis Trust, 1957)

Alice A. Bailey. *Initiation, Human and Solar* (UK, London: Lucis Trust, 1922)

Alice A. Bailey. *A Treatise on White Magic* (UK, London: Lucis Trust, 1934), 14th printing, 1979

Alice A. Bailey. *Between War and Peace* (USA, New York, NY: Lucis Press, 1942)

Alice A. Bailey. *A Treatise on the Seven Rays, Volume III – Esoteric Astrology* (UK, London: Lucis Trust, 1951), 10th printing 1975

Enrique Barrios. *Ami, Child of the Stars* (USA, Santa Fe, NM: Lotus Press, 1989)

Laurent Basset (dir.). *The Secret – Evidence We Are Not Alone* (USA: iO Productions, 2002)

Chip Berlet, 'Siren Song – Conspiracy!'. *The New Internationalist*, issue 405, October 2007

H.P. Blavatsky. 'The Dual Aspect of Wisdom', *Lucifer*, Vol. VII, No.37, 15 September 1890

H.P. Blavatsky. *The Secret Doctrine* (UK, London: The Theosophical Publishing Company, 1888). Adyar edition (India, Adyar: The Theosophical Publishing House, 1938), 6th ed., 1971

Willy Brandt (ed.). *North-South – A Programme for Survival* (USA, Cambridge, MA: The MIT Press/UK, London: Pan Books, 1980)

Stefano Breccia. *Mass Contacts* (UK, Milton Keynes: AuthorHouse, 2009)

Fritjof Capra. 'The New Physics and the Scientific Reality of our Time'. In David Lorimer (ed), *The Spirit of Science – From Experiment to Experience* (UK, Edinburgh: Floris Books, 1998)

Pier Carpi. *Le Profezie di Papa Giovanni* (Italy, Rome: Edizione Mediterranee, 1976)

Ronald Caswell. 'In Defence of Wilbert Smith', *UFO Contact*, IGAP Journal Vol.2, No.8, December 1967

Ronald Caswell. 'Wired for sound'. *UFO Contact*, IGAP Journal Vol.2, No.8, December 1967

Ivan Ceci. 'Perego, il console degli UFO', *Corriere della Sera*, 16 February 2011

Ivan Ceci. 'Witness of Italian extraterrestrial contact case emerges', ExoNews, 15 August 2011

Andy Coghlan and Debora MacKenzie. 'Revealed – the capitalist network that runs the world'. *New Scientist* magazine No.2835, 22 October 2011

Sylvia Cranston. *HPB – The Extraordinary Life and Influence of Helena Blavatsky, Founder of the Modern Theosophical Movement* (USA, New York, NY: Tarcher Putnam, 1993)

Gordon W. Creighton. 'The Italian Scene – Part 3: Bruno Ghibaudi's contact claim'. *Flying Saucer Review* Vol.9, No.3, May-June 1963

Benjamin Creme. *The Ageless Wisdom Teaching - An introduction to humanity's spiritual legacy* (USA, Los Angeles, CA: Share International, 1995)

Benjamin Creme. *The Gathering of the Forces of Light – UFOs and their Spiritual Mission* (USA, Los Angeles, CA: Share International, 2010)

Benjamin Creme. *The Great Approach – New Light and Life for Humanity* (USA, Los Angeles, CA: Share International, 2001)

Benjamin Creme. *Maitreya's Mission, Vol. Two* (USA, Los Angeles, CA: Share International, 1993)

Benjamin Creme. *Maitreya's Mission Vol. Three* (USA, Los Angeles, CA: Share International, 1997)

Benjamin Creme. *The Reappearance of the Christ and the Masters of Wisdom* (UK, London: Tara Press, 1979)

Benjamin Creme (ed.). *Share International* magazine Vol.4, No.3, March 1986; Vol.21, No.1, January/February 2002; Vol.24, No.3, April 2005; Vol.29, No.6, July/August 2010; No.8, October 2010; No.9, November 2010; No.10, December 2010; Vol.30, No.2, March 2011; No.3, April 2011; No.4, May 2011; No.6, July/August 2011

Adam Curtis (dir.). *The Trap – What Happened to Our Dream of Freedom?*, Part 2: "The Lonely Robot". (UK, London: British Broadcasting Corporation, 2007)

Richard Dawkins. *The Enemies of Reason*, episode 2: "The Irrational Health Service". (UK, London: Channel Four TV, 2007)

Pablo Dessy. '¿Seres de luz en Ongamira?', analuisacid.com, 8 August 2009

Giorgio Dibitonto. *Angels in Starships* (USA, Phoenix, AZ: UFO Photo Archives, 1990)

Nikola Duper. 'The story of "Friendship" ' (PDF, 2009)

Masaru Emoto. *Messages from Water* (The Netherlands, Ouderkerk aan de Amstel: Hado Publishing, 2003)

Ernesto de la Fuente. *Isla Friendship – Conexion OVNI* (Chile: PDF, 2001)

Paolo di Girolamo. *Noi e Loro* (Italy: Nexus Edizioni, 2009)

Timothy Good. *Above Top Secret* (UK, London: Guild Publishing, 1988)

Timothy Good. *Alien Base – Earth's Encounters with Extraterrestrials*. (UK, London: Century, 1998)

Timothy Good. *Unearthly Disclosure* (UK, London: Century, 2000)

Neil Gould. Interview with Philippe de la Mezussière (Exopolitics Hong

Kong, July 2010)

Steven Greer M.D. 'Exopolitics or Xenopolitics'. The Disclosure Project, 2 May 2006

Josep Guijarro. *Karma*-7, No.292, June 1998

Tony Halpin. 'Were Russian secrets shared with 'space alien' visitors?' (UK, London: *The Times*, 7 May 2010)

Jason Hanna, 'UFOs eyed nukes, ex-Air Force personnel say'. CNN newsblog *This Just In*, 27 September 2010

Paola Harris. 'Italy's disclosure of human looking aliens!' (2009)

Paola Harris. 'Why Me?', interview with Maurizio Cavallo (2006)

Paul Hellyer. *Light at the End of the Tunnel. A Survival Plan for the Human Species* (USA, Bloomington, IN: AuthorHouse, 2010)

Michael Hesemann (dir.). *Ships of Light – The Carlos Diaz Experience* (Germany, Düsseldorf: 2000 Film Productions, 2001)

Antonio Huneeus. 'Russian-style Exopolitics – Kirsan Ilyumzhinov's alien abduction'. Open Minds TV, 16 June 2010

Gregory Katz. 'UN Official denies she has a role representing Earth to extraterrestrials'. AP News, 5 October 2010

Ledyard King-Gannett. 'Former Air Force Officers Discuss Sightings', *Air Force Times News*, 27 September 2010

Tessa Koop. 'Tessa Koop meets Ervin László' (The Netherlands, Haarlem: Tessed Productions 2008)

David Korten. 'The Path to Real Prosperity'. *YES! Magazine*, 7 September 2011

Alexander Lauterwasser. *Water Sound Images: The Creative Music of the Universe* (USA, Berkeley, CA: Macromedia Press, 2007)

Desmond Leslie. *The Amazing Mr Lutterworth* (UK, London: Allan Wingate, 1958)

Desmond Leslie & George Adamski. *Flying Saucers Have Landed*, Revised and Enlarged edition (UK, London: Neville Spearman 1970)

Nick Margerrison. Interview with Dr Edgar Mitchell (UK, Peterborough: Kerrang! Radio, 23 July 2008)

Benjamin Creme's Master. 'A New Era Dawns'. *Share International*, Vol.1, No.6, July 1982

Benjamin Creme's Master. 'The voice of the people is heard'. *Share International*, Vol.30, No.2, March 2011

Henry S. Olcott. *Old Diary Leaves: The True Story of the Theosophical Society*, Second Series, 1878-83 (1895)

Robert Oppenheimer and Albert Einstein. 'Relationship with Inhabitants of Celestial Bodies' (Draft, 1947)

Octavio Ortiz. *Friendship – ¿Evidencias de contacto extraterrestre?* (Spain, Málaga: Ediciones Corona Borealis, 2010)

Elaine H. Pagels and Helmut Koester. 'From Jesus to Christ – the story of the storytellers: The Gospel of Thomas'. In Robert J. Miller (ed.), *The Complete Gospels* (USA, Santa Rosa, CA: Polebridge Press, 1995)

Alberto Perego. *L'aviazione di altri pianeti opera tra noi: rapporto agli italiani: 1943-1963* (Italy, Rome: Centro Italiano Studi Aviazione Elettromagnetica Roma, 1963)

Alberto Perego. *Sono Extraterrestri!* (Italy, Rome: Edizioni Alper, 1958)

Hans C. Peterson. 'In Defence of the Abductees' (Denmark, Jelling: IGAPE-RCN, n.d.)

Yogi Ramacharaka. *Lessons in Gnani Yoga – The Yoga of Wisdom.* (USA, New York, NY: Yogi Publication Society, 1909)

Wilhelm Reich. 'The Discovery of the Orgone'. In Wilhelm Reich, *Selected Writings* (USA, New York, NY: Farrar, Straus and Cudahy, 1960)

Daniel Ross (ed.). *UFOs and Space Science*, No.1, December 1989

Carl Sagan. 'Are they coming for us?'. *Parade Magazine*, March 1993

Carl Sagan. *The Demon-Haunted World* (UK, London: Headline Book Publishing, 1997)

Annemiek Schrijver. 'Het Alziend Oog', 31 December 2006. (The Netherlands, Hilversum: IKON TV, 2006)

Rupert Sheldrake Ph.D. *A New Science of Life – The Hypothesis of Formative Causation* (UK, London: Blond & Briggs, 1981)

Wilbert B. Smith. Speech given 31 March 1958 in Ottowa, Canada. *Flying Saucer Review* Vol.9, No.5, September-October 1963.

Wilbert B. Smith. 'Binding Forces'. *Flying Saucer Review*, Vol.7, No.2, March-April 1961

Wilbert B. Smith. *The Boys from Topside.* (USA, Clarksburg, WV: Saucerian Books, 1969)

Wilbert B. Smith. 'Official Reticence'. *Flying Saucer Review*, Vol.6, No.3, May-June 1960

Wilbert B. Smith. 'The Philosophy of the Saucers' (n.d.), <www.presidentialufo.com>

Televisión Nacional de Chile (TVN). *La Isla de Friendship*, 1999

Luca Trovellesi Cesana (dir.). *Il Caso Amicizia* (Italy: Studio3TV, 2010)

David Whitehouse. 'Is anybody out there – with a soul?'. *The Independent*, 3 November 2010

Michael Wolf. *The Catchers of Heaven.* (USA, Pittsburgh, PA: Dorrance Publishing, 1993), 2nd printing 1996

Vera P. Zelihovsky. 'A Spectre Guide'. *The Theosophist*, Vol.I, No.10, July 1880

Lou Zinsstag & Timothy Good. *George Adamski – The Untold Story* (UK, Beckenham: CETI Publications, 1983)

INDEX